PROBLEM HUNTER

PROBLEM HUNTER

BECOME THE
MOST VALUABLE PERSON
IN ANY ORGANISATION

CRAIG CALDER

Copyright © 2025 Craig Calder

All rights reserved.

No part of this book may be reproduced in any form without prior permission from the author, except as permitted by Australian copyright law.

ISBN: 978-1-7638077-1-6

This is a work of non-fiction. However, some of the names and personal characteristics of the individuals involved and contributions provided have, in some cases, been changed to disguise and protect their identities.

Although the author has made every effort to ensure that the information and references in this book were correct at the time of publication, the author assumes no responsibility for errors, inaccuracies or omissions and disclaims any liability to any party for any loss, damage, or disruption caused by errors or omissions.

The information contained in this book is of a general nature only. Readers should not rely on the general information in this book as a substitute for expert professional advice and services where required. Readers accept that results will vary depending on the level of skill and expertise of those using the methods and strategies contained in this book.

A catalogue record for this work is available from the National Library of Australia.

Publisher: Hembury Books

Cover design: Bettina Kaiser

The path to freedom is to find and solve problems that matter.

Comfort is an illusion of the mind that keeps us weak.

It takes the courage of only one person to change an entire system.

Your creativity does not have an expiry date.

Tension fuels progress.

Your value multiplies by creating better.

Definitions

Problem
A difficult situation that needs a solution to achieve something important.
There are plenty of them in every organisation.

Hunter
Someone who intentionally pursues important things.
Such as a bargain hunter, treasure hunter or job hunter.

Problem Hunter
Someone who intentionally pursues challenging problems and solves them.
The most valuable person in any organisation.

Contents

Introduction..1

Section 1: A Problem Hunter's Perspective.....................9
1. The MVPs in any organisation.............................11
2. A job is just a temporary solution.......................21
3. Paradise of problems.....................................25
4. Perspective intelligence.................................33
5. Failure is just feedback.................................49

Section 2: A Problem Hunter's Mindset........................59
6. Problems create leaders..................................61
7. Turd observing stinks....................................69
8. Beware your Judgement Junkie............................75
9. Mindset Reset..85
10. Sidestep these thinking traps..........................109
11. Prevent 'Dark Marks'...................................123

Section 3: A Problem Hunter's Strategy......................129
12. Understand the Reason..................................133
13. Choose the Result......................................153
14. Develop the Response (Part 1)..........................167
15. Develop the Response (Part 2)..........................191
16. Find help that propels you forward....................213
17. Choose the opposite way................................221

Section 4: A Problem Hunter's Capabilities..................231
18. Pathfinding..235
19. Connecting...245
20. Producing..259
21. Tasking..267
22. Learn to learn faster..................................279
23. Multitasking isn't always smart........................289

Conclusion..295

Acknowledgements..296

About the Author..300

Endnotes..301

Introduction

I used to think problems were universally bad news and should be avoided whenever possible. It seemed smart to navigate my life and career by always staying away from 'trouble' or difficult situations. But this approach backfired. And, as I have learned, will always backfire. Within the space of 12 months when I was in my early forties, I had lost my job, my marriage and, as a result, my sense of self. I was lost and desperately searching for answers.

As I took stock of my life and how I had led it up to that point, I realised I had become an expert at *spotting and steering clear* of difficult problems but was wilfully blind to how important it is to do the work to *solve* them. Instead of hunting for challenging problems and walking the path to directly address them, I stayed stuck and vulnerable by choosing to ignore or avoid them. As a cycling buddy used to tell me, "You don't get good at the things you never train for". I wish I had listened more closely to that advice.

So why write this book? What is it about? And why should you consider reading it? Good questions to ask. Let me try and answer them for you.

This book is the result of 25 years' experience and research into what makes people exceptional at problem-solving—and how they do it. And why learning how to solve challenging problems is one of the greatest investments you can make in yourself. I wrote this book to capture the lessons and methods I have learned about problem-solving and to share them in the hope it provides insight and support for people who have found themselves in similar situations to me.

Ask any successful business leader, entrepreneur, and even politician, and they will tell you problems create great opportunities. People who become experts at finding and solving challenging problems become the most valuable people in any organisation. Organisations that develop exceptional collective problem-solving capabilities become titans in their industry.

My first career was as a management consultant for the global consulting firm EY. My speciality was providing clients with advice on where their biggest risks and potential problems were and offering strategies for how they could prevent or solve them.

My job was to shine a light on the big things that could cause major disruption before they happened so they could be avoided. As a consultant, I was trained to see other people's problems, but not do the work to solve them.

Working in a global consulting firm was something I loved doing, but I also felt a knot inside my stomach because I wasn't learning what I needed to learn. I wanted to broaden my skills and experience, but at the time didn't really know what I wanted or needed to do. Like any big business, the larger it becomes, the more specialised it needs its employees to be. I had become very specialised in what I did, and I didn't know how to find a path from what I was doing that would help reinvigorate my career.

Feelings of guilt and failure clouded my thinking and prevented me from having open and honest conversations with the leaders of the firm about how I was feeling at that time, which was burned out. I was isolated by my thoughts and believed I had no other option than to leave to dull the pain of burnout.

After leaving EY, I joined a large company as their Chief Risk Officer. It's a job that also involves looking for problems and suggesting strategies for others to solve them. I was essentially a professional problem-finder, doing similar work to what I did at EY, but with only one 'client'.

It was intellectually stimulating, but it didn't solve my core problem. My solution, to change jobs to arrest feelings of burnout, had failed. A restructure within the business resulted in me being let go from this job after three years. I was suddenly middle aged, out of work and lacking purpose and direction.

Amidst my professional turmoil, my personal life was also unravelling. My marriage was in crisis. My then wife and I had been to three different marriage counsellors, attended many counselling sessions together and separately, and tried as best we could to understand and find a path to solve the hurt and differences we had with each other. But it didn't work. A 13-year marriage ended because we couldn't find a solution that worked for us both. I had never thought I would end up in this situation. In fact, I feared it more than anything else.

We had two young children, and I was devastated at the thought of not being able to wake with them each morning. We had no major conflicts, but we had grown distant, allowed too much unhealed hurt to accumulate and as a result had both emotionally shut down. Problems remain stuck when you fear a potential solution. Fear immobilises you from acting, which often leads to a worse outcome than if you had acted sooner.

This period of my life caused me to learn the hard way about the true value of problems and the importance of being proactive towards solving and learning from them, rather than avoiding them. What I came to realise was that while I had become skilled at spotting problems and advising others how to solve them, I had let my own skills of *actually solving them* remain underdeveloped. And this had contributed to my predicament. It's like learning all the moves of a game but never actually playing it—no matter how well you know the rules, real capability only comes from being in the game and developing yourself through real situations.

When you feel vulnerable, your mind works to protect you by avoiding what it considers threatening. I didn't realise it, but my mind was working against me to avoid taking steps to solve the biggest problems I had, because I didn't have the confidence, know-how and skills to solve them.

Problems are difficult situations that need solutions to make things better, not just inconveniences to be ignored. What makes a problem significant or challenging is that it is hard to understand, has high stakes, and there are no simple or known solutions. Problems create a gap between now and a future we prefer. What gives problems meaning is the perspective through which we choose to see them and the beliefs that influence our judgement and actions towards them.

I had constructed a life that allowed me to dodge the discomfort and challenge of the most significant problems I had. I had unconscious beliefs that undermined how I thought and acted, that kept me trapped seeking comfort and avoidance. Without realising it, I had let myself become a passenger to the biggest problems in my life, both personally and professionally.

Problems always seem much bigger when you are unprepared to manage them. A lifeguard at Bondi Beach once told me, "When you're caught in a rip while swimming you don't blame the ocean, you focus on how you're going to get yourself back to safety". Knowing how to swim gives you an advantage to survive when you get caught in a rip. Knowing how to solve problems in a workplace gives you an advantage to survive when they are thrown at you, and to thrive when you seek them out.

How I learned the secrets and value of problem-solving

After being let go from my corporate job, I started a journey to learn as much as I could about solving challenging problems. I knew how to *spot* them, but I wanted to experience how to *solve* them.

I established a consulting business, ThinkClear Group, in 2012, with the intention of supporting clients to solve challenging problems and use the experiences to develop a holistic approach to problem-solving that could help others. I sought out client work that required me to take on increasingly more responsibility for directly solving complex problems. I led property development teams, implemented technological transformations, found technology solutions to create efficiencies and cost savings, managed corporate insurance claims litigation, supported corporate mergers and acquisitions, and directed teams to capture post-merger integration cost savings and improvements. I learned from an exceptional group of people I worked with and developed an understanding and appreciation for how a diverse range of complex problems are understood and solved within demanding constraints.

Six years ago, I started a commercial art business creating and selling abstract paintings and sculptures to collectors. The problem-solving strategies used by artists can be directly applied to how we tackle challenges in any workplace. In fact, by studying art, I learned one of the most versatile problem-solving strategies that's been used for thousands of years: inversion. It's where you choose to see a problem from the opposite perspective to spark creative solutions.

Each of the experiences I've had has helped shape my thoughts on the value of problems in our lives and how to relate to them and find ways to show up and solve them. I discovered the people who see problems as the path of progress are the ones that leap ahead. They are the alchemists within an organisation – able to turn a difficult situation into something of great value.

To write this book, I combined my experience in spotting and solving problems with the wisdom of a wide variety of people who had all developed their own clever ways to understand and solve problems. They included architects, artists, business leaders, cancer survivors, company board members, educators, engineers, entrepreneurs, filmmakers, management consultants, marketers, medical specialists, neuroscientists, psychologists, recruiters, sales professionals, and social entrepreneurs. Some were still in their youth, some in middle age and some much older and wiser than me. I also pored over available problem-solving literature and research from psychology, neuroscience, mathematics, philosophy, medicine, business and the arts to find common insights to draw from.

To develop our problem-solving expertise, we need to master important aspects of both our internal and external worlds. Our *internal world* is the perspectives and mindset we adopt that help us see and experience problems and shape the meaning and motivation we attribute to them. Our *external world* is the tangible strategies, skills and approach to learning that support us to find and engage with problems.

In other words, to become a great problem-solver you need to master *how you think and feel* about problems as well as learning *what you do* to find and solve them. Problems challenge our sense of self as much as our ability to solve them. Most of us develop our problem-solving skills and wisdom through experience. Some of us have had problem-solving training, but it's not common. Usually, problem-solving is taught within a specific context such marketing, finance, communication or relationships.

We learn the hacks and ways of thinking others have used to solve these specific problems, but don't often learn how to become great at solving any problem. I was taught how to solve finance and business-specific problems at university, and later while working as a management consultant. When we stop seeking out new problems to solve, we unintentionally risk career stagnation and burnout. Solving new problems helps us grow our skills and show the added value we bring, which leads to more opportunities.

Problem Hunter

What I noticed about people who were masters at solving problems was they didn't sit back and wait for new and challenging problems to come to them. They hunted for them. Just as you would hunt for a house, hunt for buried treasure, hunt for a job or hunt for a bargain. They were intentional about finding challenging problems to work on.

And when they found one, they hunted for a solution. They knew the value to them and their organisation was in solving a problem, not just pointing it out. That's how the idea of a Problem Hunter was born.

A Problem Hunter is a person who intentionally pursues challenging problems and solves them. As a result, they become the most valuable people in any organisation. They are the engines of innovation and primers of high-performing teams because they choose to take action and lead when others wait for instructions.

Who this book is for

If you're looking for a guide to help you create new thinking, skills and experience to propel your career forward, this book is for you.

If you feel stuck in your career and progress has stalled and you're searching for a path to become unstuck, this book is for you.

If you're working on a challenging problem and are searching for inspiration and insights to help you discover how to think differently about it so you can take further steps to solve it, this book is for you.

If you're a leader and want to transform your team into expert problem-solvers to achieve more, this book is also for you.

Problem Hunter is ultimately a book about freedom. Freedom to think objectively and independently, freedom to pursue challenges that will bring you satisfaction and reward, and freedom to make choices and pursue the type of work that creates the life you want to live.

What's in this book and how it can help you

Problem Hunter is divided into four sections.

In the first section, A Problem Hunter's Perspective, I illustrate how people who develop high levels of problem-solving expertise become the most valuable people in any organisation. How they see problems, their perspectives, gives them extraordinary vision and clarity. We may not all be able to see this way at first. But with increased awareness using the Perspective IQ Framework, anyone can shift their focus to see problems more clearly and open up a broader range of previously unseen possibilities.

The second section, A Problem Hunter's Mindset, explains how the internal world of our thoughts, beliefs and emotions can become invisible barriers that subconsciously hold us back. It provides a simple way to expose and overcome them: the Mindset Reset method.

The third section, A Problem Hunter's Strategy, shares a three-step method and 10 actions that will help you better understand and solve any workplace problem. I call it the 3R Problem Solving Strategy. It's framed around understanding the *Reason* you have a problem, the *Result* you want to achieve and deciding the best *Response* to solve it.

The fourth section, A Problem Hunter's Capabilities, unpacks four essential problem-solving capabilities and the skills and beliefs needed to master them. The four essential capabilities are pathfinding, connecting, producing and tasking.

Each section has case studies and examples illustrating how others have solved problems or explaining how to use the methods and strategies included in this book. Some case studies provide inspiring success stories and others are monumental screw-ups. We learn from both! At the end of each chapter is a summary of key points. I call these Hunting Tips.

My intention with this book is to provide you with a set of simple ideas and practical tools to help you become the most valuable person in any organisation—a Problem Hunter.

Craig Calder

Sydney, Australia, 2025

A Problem Hunter's Perspective

OVERVIEW

A perspective is a specific viewpoint or angle from which someone perceives, interprets and understands a situation, event or idea. Our perspectives are like lenses that colour our view of events, people and challenges in the moment. It's part of the mental framework through which we make sense of the world around us, shaping our reactions, decisions and attitudes.

Perspective always precedes action. How we see and interpret situations directly influences what we do about them. In problem-solving, perspective plays a key role in determining which aspects of a problem are emphasised, how the problem is approached and discussed, what solutions are considered or ignored and, ultimately, how effectively they are addressed.

What I've observed in people who excel at problem-solving is that they're highly aware of their own default perspectives and how these influence their thinking and actions, as well as the thoughts and actions of others. They can adjust their perspective to suit the specific situation, seeing problems as opportunities for growth and value creation, both for themselves and the organisations they work with. They see a business as a paradise of problems to engage with, where each job is just a temporary solution, and every failure is simply feedback along the path to developing innovations and creating change that matters.

In this section, we explore how perspective is a powerful tool in your problem-solving kitbag and provide you with a method, the Perspective IQ framework, that helps make yours more adaptable and effective in each situation.

CHAPTER 1

The MVPs in any organisation

"Strive not to be a success, but rather to be of value."
Albert Einstein

Why do some people stand out more than others in the workplace? It's not because of their titles or the number of years they've spent with the company, but because of their ability to get the right things done. That creates value. What underpins this capability is the ability to proactively identify and solve the challenging problems that unlock value.

Problems create opportunity. They are the lifeblood of a business and the waves that careers are surfed on. People who solve the most valuable problems become the most valuable people (MVP) in any organisation because they are the engines of progress, innovation and resilience. Their value goes far beyond just being more productive—they are the linchpins that keep an organisation adaptive, competitive and forward-moving.

They are the people fought over for recruitment. The leader of a global recruitment agency told me the most sought-after attribute of senior leaders he recruits is agility. Which is the ability to spot where problems are or where they could be and lead an organisation to find solutions to them that protect and create value. Being smart is not enough. Being hardworking is not enough. Being loyal is not enough. Being capable of seeing where problems are and taking action to protect or capitalise on them is how people become more valuable in any organisation. And these attributes can be developed by anyone. These people are Problem Hunters.

The source of their value

To understand why Problem Hunters are so valuable, let's first explore what makes them unique. A Problem Hunter's perspective is not to wait for problems to land on their desk; they actively seek out potential issues, challenges or areas for improvement and take ownership of finding solutions. Their perspective is not reactive, where action is only taken when a problem becomes urgent. Instead, it's anticipatory, focusing on preventing issues before they escalate or identifying opportunities that others might overlook.

Working in any organisation means having a role with specific responsibilities and boundaries. Problem Hunters can see beyond the manufactured walls of their role and make connections to how the organisation can better serve its customers, create efficiencies that improve profitability, spot gaps that create a risk of exposure to future loss and prevent it, and cultivate their curiosity to create ideas that spark innovation.

Problem Hunters make a choice—to find a path that brings challenge and opportunity and contributes to making things better. They choose to not just do what's asked of them, they find the space and time to explore and make things better. They use problems as their vehicle to propel them forward.

They drive innovation

Innovation starts out as an itch or a desire. Something that's not right that needs improving or doesn't exist and needs to be created. It starts with seeing a problem, a gap from now to a desired better future, and taking the reins to solve it.

Professor Fred Hollows was an Australian eye surgeon and humanitarian who discovered the widespread problem of cataracts causing treatable blindness during his work with Indigenous communities in Australia and impoverished regions around the world.

In 1968, after treating two Aboriginal men in his eye clinic, Fred was invited to visit their Wattie Creek camp in the Northern Territory. What he saw was shocking—poor health conditions, especially in eye care, that left him stunned. He couldn't believe people in Australia were living like this.

What disturbed him most was the large number of children and adults suffering from trachoma, a disease that causes blindness, rarely found in other parts of the country. He visited a number of other Aboriginal communities and found the same problem. The problem he found was that cataract surgery was either unavailable or too expensive, making accessible eye care almost impossible for people living in these communities. Without someone driving change, people would continue to needlessly become blind and suffer a terribly poor quality of life as a result. Nine out of 10 people become blind needlessly.

To solve this problem, Hollows developed low-cost, high-quality intraocular lenses, and trained local doctors and health care workers to perform cataract surgeries. This made the treatment both affordable and sustainable. Sight can now be restored through cataract surgery for as little as $25. Hollows said, "Individuals can and must help. Look at the problem and do something, don't just sit back". Through his direct work and the work of others, his foundation has helped restore sight to over 150 million people worldwide and built local capacity across 25 countries to address the issue long-term.[1]

Problem Hunters see problems as a path to help people and don't wait for others to act. They use innovation as their path to create change that helps others.

They lift team performance

Choosing to be proactive, choosing to run towards problems that need to be addressed, takes a moment of courage and it's a conscious decision. Every day we make over 30,000 choices, from the time we wake to the moment we turn off the lights and fall asleep. That's one decision every two seconds (assuming we sleep for eight hours). Most choices we've made thousands of times before, to help us do the basics of living, such as walking, eating and communicating.

Our subconscious mind makes 95% of our choices each day.[2] Meaning we aren't aware of most choices we make, even when we are conscious. The reason for this is our brains create habits and routines to conserve energy. We stay in these routines until we consciously change them.

If we see someone who is acting differently, being proactive, creating results we would like to achieve by doing things differently to how we are doing them, we become motivated to follow. It causes us to consciously think about changing ourselves to achieve more. This behaviour is referred to by psychologists as vicarious reinforcement, where we choose to imitate others when we respect the person involved or see them achieve positive outcomes. When someone chooses to act courageously, to run towards a problem and solve it, it can break the social and psychological barriers that hold others back.

Problem Hunters help others make better choices. There is nothing more motivating than working with people who are eager to succeed. It sets a standard you can see and wakes people up from a work routine slumber that is awl too easy to fall into. Problem Hunters create a team culture that thrives.

Problem Hunting programs

Some organisations cultivate Problem Hunters, knowing they will produce significant value.

3M's 15% program encourages employees to set aside a portion of their work time to proactively work on ideas and problems that excite them.[3] This initiative has led to the development of many innovations, including multilayer optical film, APC Flash-Free Adhesive and the ubiquitous Post-it Notes. The program encourages employees to seek out and solve problems that interest them in creative ways.

Engineers at W. L. Gore & Associates created Elixir guitar strings from a program they called 'dabble time', where associates take time to think about problem-solving or creating products of value.[4] In the early 1990s, a small crew of engineers was working on creating cables that controlled the movements of Disney animatronics which they found difficult to handle. Their solution was to develop a smoother, lower-friction cable using a polymer-based coating.

One of the engineers was a guitar player. Working with these cables, he noticed how similar they were to guitar strings. He wondered if the polymer coating would improve the quality of guitar strings which were made of similar materials to cables controlling the animatronics. Using his 'dabble time', he found the polymer coating kept guitar strings in a 'like new' state for much longer compared to other strings. Elixir is now a leading brand of guitar strings sold worldwide.

Next Jump, a leadership development and decision-making training organisation, has a program for new hires that includes engaging in a 'plus-1 project'.[5] New recruits are challenged to identify one way to improve the customer service process as part of their training. They need to find a problem and develop a solution to graduate from their orientation boot camp.

While some companies actively encourage and create Problem Hunters, you can create your own environment to seek out new problems to solve by remaining curious about how the business you work in works, what problems it helps customers solve and letting your creativity ask, "How can it be better?".

The danger of comfort

Doing what we have always done creates a sense of comfort and control. Doing challenging and new things takes energy to overcome uncertainty. Our brains want us to seek comfort in order to conserve energy, and to pursue familiar activities as a substitute for development, keeping us distracted. But it comes at a significant cost if we aren't careful. Your career comfort zone should be a temporary rest stop, not a permanent destination.

Harvard professors Robert Keegan and Lisa Lahey are experts in adult development. Their research found that, "The single biggest cause of work burnout is not work overload but working too long without experiencing your own personal development".[6]

If you work more than two years without learning something new, taking on a new challenge or responsibility, you will likely start to feel some effects of burnout. Without significant learning, you might start to notice that you become disengaged, bored, start to complain and see far more small irritations in your workplace that bother you.

As a result, your satisfaction at work will most likely start to plummet. When this happens, it's understandable to start thinking it's the job's fault and blame the organisation for not preventing you from feeling this way.

Your career comfort zone should be a temporary rest stop, not a permanent destination.

People often quit jobs in the hope that the pain of burnout through lack of development will go away if they change their environment. I've done this, not believing I had any other options. If you are considering a job or employer change because you feel burned out, before you take action, consider finding a challenging problem to solve as a strategy to rediscover motivation and energy for your current workplace.

Problems that require us to learn new things and persevere through the messiness of creating and implementing a novel solution are the perfect playground for your development. Later in the book I show you how to find problems to work on using the problem tree method. Your colleagues or managers may also have many of them to choose from. Showing initiative will help you stand out.

If you don't have to solve new and challenging problems in your current role, volunteering for one can feel a little uncomfortable at first. But persist with it. The discomfort you feel is a trick of your mind. Discomfort is a necessary part of growth. Taking steps to seek out and solve new and challenging problems in your workplace is a way to stay engaged, develop new skills and make yourself more valuable. It's important to have a steady stream of new problems to feed on.

For some people, however, burnout needs a more radical solution when too much time has passed without new problems to drive their development. Marc Gregory had built a marketing agency in his native South Africa over 15 years, employing 35 people with global brand name clients that included Coca-Cola and L'Oreal. His business was the leader in the youth marketing sector he specialised in. By the time he reached his late 30s he had developed acute work burnout that culminated in spending time in hospital to recover.

He said to me of this time, "I'd just fallen out of love with my business, and I knew I wanted to change. I just didn't know what the change looked like." Despite feeling something wasn't right, Marc kept doing more of the same. "I just continued to tough it out in the business. I took on more responsibility and I was ignoring the messages my body was giving me until I couldn't ignore them any longer."

Reflecting on that time, Marc realised he hadn't done any deep learning or self-development for many years. "It had been maybe five to 10 years since I learned something new", he told me. "I was probably quite stuck. I was on autopilot."

It had been too long without deep development work for Marc to recover his passion for the business. After recovering from his hospital visit, he chose to sell his marketing business and start anew. He decided to do something completely different to wake up what had been left undeveloped within.

Marc established a business creating a new type of photographic portraiture, called Purpose Portraits, that blended his passion for digital art with traditional photography to bring out the essence and purpose of his clients. His work is unique and intensely rewarding, he told me. This new business provided the steady stream of new meaningful problems to solve that reignited his passion for work.

Most people who change careers do so at age 39.[7] The most common cause is feeling their careers have stagnated. Careers stagnate when either there are no further roles to fill that advance your career or you don't work on new opportunities to expand your capabilities and value.

"Business opportunities are like buses, there's always another one coming", Richard Branson says. "The key is having the right people to seize those opportunities and solve the problems that arise." Make it your priority to become one of the *right people* to help seize new opportunities. Be one of the *right people* in your organisation by becoming a Problem Hunter.

Seeking out new, challenging problems within your organisation to solve will keep you safe from the effects of career burnout through lack of continuous development. It will also position you for more opportunities in the future. It will help you become one of the MVPs within your organisation.

CHAPTER 1

The MVPs in any organisation

- People are valued more when they routinely identify and solve significant probles. These people are Problem Hunters.
- Problem Hunters are proactive and accountable, and foster engaging, innovative and productive cultures.
- Becoming a Problem Hunter not only creates value for you and your organisation, it's also a powerful antidote to career burnout.

CHAPTER 2

A job is just a temporary solution

"All is flux, nothing stays still."
Heraclitus

I came close to losing my first job not long after I started. It was only luck that saved me. I learned quickly no job is ever permanent, and it's not meant to be.

I landed my first full-time job in my early 20s, as an accountant in a medium-sized audit and consulting firm called Duesburys. It was acquired by Deloitte, the global consulting firm, years later. I started work with seven other graduates my age. I earned enough money to cover my rent, food, entertainment and have a bit left over. Perfect, I thought! My first job was to audit a client's financial records and annual financial reports to make sure they were true and fairly presented.

Three months after starting, I was called to attend a meeting early one Monday morning with three of my graduate colleagues. I thought something was a bit strange when the senior staff and partners in the meeting room all had long faces when we walked in.

> A job is just a temporary solution to a current business problem.

The managing partner at the time stood at the head of the boardroom and said, "The economy is headed for recession, and we don't think client demand will be as strong as we thought it would be six months ago. So unfortunately, we had to let four of your colleagues go."

I was grateful I had been spared but devastated for my new friends at the same time. I hadn't given a second thought to the possibility that my employer might choose to let some of us go. The story I told myself was that things had been so good for so long, why would there ever be a reason for that to change? I was in my twenties at the time and very naïve.

The partners of my firm had made the rational decision of cutting costs so they wouldn't run into financial difficulty. A professional services firm, like any business, is just a balancing act between cash coming in and cash going out. If you don't have enough money coming in to cover expenses, you need to cut costs.

What I learned from this experience is that a job is just a *temporary solution* to a *current problem* a business or organisation has. And that is how it's meant to be.

When my employer hired eight graduates, they believed their current problem of serving new clients over the next year was enough to need all eight of us as the solution.

However, when the economy contracted suddenly, the size of the problem they had originally solved for by hiring eight graduates was much smaller. In fact, half the size they had originally thought. When a current problem no longer exists, or in this example, is reduced in size, the solution to solve it must also change to match.

This experience helped shift my perspective on the role of jobs in the workforce. I had let myself initially think my job was 'safe' because I was a 'permanent hire'. After half of my colleagues were suddenly made redundant, I realised that all jobs are only ever temporary because a business only needs jobs when those jobs fulfil a purpose.

A job's purpose is to solve a current business problem. And when that problem changes or goes away, the rational decision is for the job to be removed too. Of course, there are employment laws that protect us from unfair workplace practices, but where alternatives can't be found, there are no options other than removing a job that isn't needed. This realisation made me feel, strangely, much better. Letting go of the belief that jobs are supposed to be 'safe' made me focus on how I could become more valuable through finding problems I could help solve and that would develop my skills and capabilities.

Nothing is meant to be permanent

The World Economic Forum[8] has forecast over the four years to 2027 that 23% of jobs will change—both new jobs created, and existing jobs replaced. New artificial intelligence technology is one of the driving forces for these changes.

We know nature follows a cycle: a beginning, a middle and, inevitably, an end. Flower buds sprout in spring, bloom in summer and return to the soil in autumn. Despite not always wanting them to, our bodies shift and change each day and noticeably each year. Change is an undeniable truth in the world we live in.

Change is simply moving from one state to another. It's a progression from present to future. It's meant to happen to all things. If change in the workplace and in life is to be expected, then the smartest thing we can do is learn how to become experts at adapting to and creating change. And this is the core of what problem-solving is: creating change that delivers improvement and minimises the difference between one state and another.

CHAPTER 2

A job is a temporary solution

- A job is a temporary solution to a current business problem and will always be subject to change.
- Change is inevitable and creates new problems that create opportunity and drive growth and development.
- Mastering the skill of identifying and solving problems prepares you to better manage and take advantage of change.

CHAPTER 3

Paradise of problems

"At its core, every business is a pipeline of value creation through solutions to problems."
David Allen

When Josephine Cochran had finished entertaining guests with her husband, William, one evening in their Shelbyville, Illinois family home, she noticed something that bothered her. As the dishes were being washed and packed away, she saw small scrapes and chips had formed around the edges of some of the plates. This was in 1870, when dishes were washed solely by hand.[9]

Despite being very careful, the process of putting plates in the sink, scrubbing them clean and placing them on drying racks or using a towel to dry them would inevitably cause some of the plates to bump together or make contact with a hard surface, causing chips to appear at the edges. This observation sparked a shift in Cochran's thinking. Instead of seeing a problem and just being annoyed, she became curious and asked herself a question, "How can I find a better way of washing the dishes without damaging them?" Her plates were family heirlooms and protecting them was important to her.

Cochran began hunting for a solution to her plate-cleaning problem shortly thereafter. No other suitable alternatives were available, so she decided to create an entirely new solution herself. Her grandfather, John Fitch, was an inventor known for his steamboat-related innovations. Her perspective on the problem wasn't that it was just an annoyance to be endured. It provided an opportunity to create something better. She chose to focus on the satisfaction of finding a solution. The pain of the problem just provided the first step of motivation towards getting there.

Cochran prepared prototype designs, and with the assistance of George Butters, a skilled mechanic, built the world's first dishwasher in a shed located behind her family home in 1885. What started as a problem became an opportunity that led Cochran to pioneer an industry that went on to revolutionise a task performed in every household, restaurant and hotel around the world. In Australia and the US around half of all households have a dishwasher[10], and in Europe over 60% of households have one. Cochrane's company eventually became KitchenAid, which was later acquired by the Whirlpool Corporation.

What Cochran did was introduce something new, a new solution that solved a current problem. She took on the challenge of finding solutions that combined to create a product that addressed a current problem she and millions of others had. That's what a business, at its most fundamental level, is: a collection of problems and solutions that combine to create products and services that benefit others. A business is literally a *paradise of problems*. They exist to solve customer problems at scale.

The problem tree

It's common to think of a business in terms of processes, people and technology or departments and functions. But the purpose behind each is the problems that have to be solved and combined to create a product or service (solution) that can be provided to a customer. We can often get confused about what a business really does by not seeing clearly what problems it solves for its customers and the cascade of problems and solutions that the business takes on to provide the service or product a customer needs.

If you want to hunt for problems to solve within the organisation you're working for, create a problem tree to help you see them clearly.

A problem tree is a method I use to simplify a business into a collection of problems and solutions to help me understand it quickly and find opportunities to help. Here's how it works.

There are five steps to creating a problem tree:

1. Choose a customer's problem and the solution your business provides that relates most closely to what you do.
2. Identify the problems your business needs to solve to deliver the solution to the customer.
3. List the primary solutions that your business undertakes to solve these problems.
4. Continue listing problems underneath solutions until you reach your role.
5. List the problems you have to solve to create the solutions your role is required to provide.

Where your role is supported by other parts of the business, continue the problem tree to show the problems you have that others solve for you. Understanding a business this way frees up your mind from just focusing on what is done today to what can be done better in future and how it can connect to other problems you help solve.

Here's an example of the basics of a problem tree for providing a dishwasher to a customer.

> **A business is literally a paradise of problems. They exist to solve customer problems at scale.**

Customer's problem: handwashing dishes takes too long and causes damage.
Solution: a dishwasher that automates washing dishes while protecting them from damage.
Problems to solve: design dishwasher, manufacture dishwasher, sell dishwasher, deliver and service dishwasher and run the business.

You can usually break a business into between five and seven major problems it has to solve. Note: I use 'Run the business' as a catch-all for all the corporate support functions, such as how to employ and remunerate people (HR), how to record transactions and prepare financial reports (Finance), how to receive payments, pay suppliers and fund the business (Treasury) and how to make the workplace safe (Safety).

Primary solutions to problems: Let's take 'Design dishwasher' as the problem we need solutions for. To design a dishwasher, in simple terms you will need to develop specifications, create prototype and test and refine prototype. There are a lot of further problems and solutions that need to be worked through to make each of these solutions work. But I hope you get the idea.

My role: I conduct prototype testing of new product designs and identify issues for the design team to rectify.

A pro tip for creating your problem tree is to use the verb–noun combination to describe your problem and solution. A problem is something you *have* to solve (action) and a solution is *how* you solve it (action). The verb–noun combination is a shortcut way of describing an action, such as Design (verb) Dishwasher (noun).

Making this visual is the best way I find to create a problem tree. Here's an example of how I would start to create one for developing and selling a dishwasher:

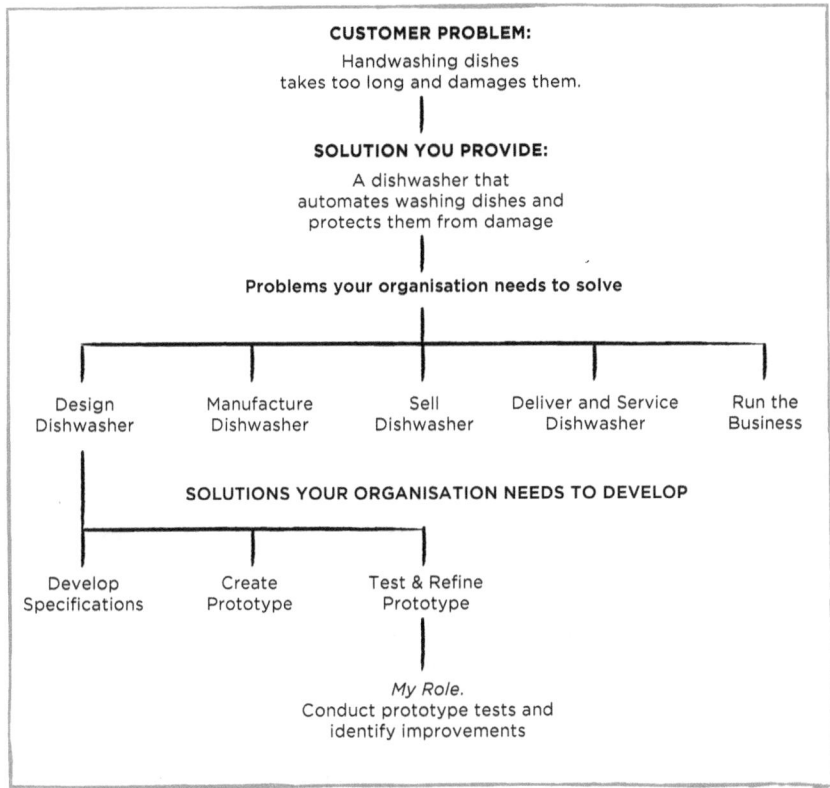

As you move down the tree, you will naturally create new branches with more problems and solutions.

When I'm trying to understand how a business works and its problems and solutions, I ask four questions:

1. What is the starting point for this part of the business? (In other words, what is the problem they start with? There may be multiple problems which you can group together.)
2. What do you need to make sure happens? (In other words, what solutions do you provide that helps the business or its customers?)
3. How do you do that? (This provides what you need to start searching for clues on how to make things better later.)

4. Is what I'm doing the only option, or could it be done better (faster, cheaper, more reliably)? This provides you with the context to improve the solutions you provide. I've come across many work practices that didn't need to be performed at all, but continued because they had always been done.

Creating problem trees helps you discover ideas and opportunities to work on. They connect you more closely to the real purpose of a business. They allow you to see more clearly how your role provides solutions that help create, sell and deliver products and services to your business's customers.

I once created a problem tree for the service department of European car dealership. They were looking for efficiencies in how their operations worked and asked for my help. After completing the problem tree and presenting it on a page to Helmut, the German leader of the service department, he said "Finally, I understand how this whole place works, now let's find opportunities to make it work better".

Solving problems that matter is the best kind of work

Everyone wants to do work they find interesting. Interesting work is where our brains are challenged through solving problems we haven't solved before, and it achieves something we consider meaningful and important. Doing interesting work that solves meaningful problems creates the best jobs people say they have ever had.[11]

Ed Catmull co-founded Pixar Animation Studios and was its president for 33 years. He was also president of Walt Disney Animation Studios for 13 years. He helped shape Pixar into a world-leading innovator in digitally animated movies, producing multiple smash hits including *Toy Story*, *Monsters, Inc.*, *The Incredibles*, *Cars* and *Finding Nemo*. Fifteen of Pixar's movies are included in the 50 highest-grossing animated feature films of all time.

He said of his time working at Pixar what made it special was that "We acknowledge we will always have problems, many of them hidden from our view; that we work hard to uncover these problems, even if doing so means making ourselves uncomfortable; and that, when we come across a problem, we marshal all of our energies to solve it. This, more than any elaborate party or turreted workstation, is why I love coming to work in the morning. It is what motivates me and gives me a sense of mission".[12]

Imagine if there were more people hunting for hidden problems and supporting each other to learn how to solve them and not come to work to 'just do a job'? Imagine your entire workplace thought like Ed Catmull and the team at Pixar and saw problems as opportunities that everyone rallied around to solve? Where working on challenging problems is a source of pride and motivation. That's a culture I want to be part of every day of the week.

CHAPTER 3

A paradise of problems

- A business exists to solve problems at scale. It is a paradise of problems and solutions that you can create opportunities from.
- Creating problem trees for a business simplifies how it works and helps stimulate ideas to innovate and create better solutions, positioning you to become more valuable.
- Solving challenging problems that matter is the most rewarding and satisfying work to do.

CHAPTER 4

Perspective intelligence

"We see things not as they are, but as we are conditioned to see them."
Immanuel Kant

"What's your perspective?" is a familiar question I receive as a consultant supporting business leaders in working through challenging problems. A new leader of a large business that employed over 3,000 people once asked me what my perspective was on whether he should be in the business of owning and operating light aircraft to transport his employees to work on mining sites in remote locations across Northern and Central Australia.

He was nervous about the safety risks and, not having had experience leading a business that operated aircraft before, he wanted to be sure it was the right thing to be doing. His perspective was that the problem was an obstacle needing immediate action. From the tone of the briefing I received, he was very cautious of the situation and wanted to know all the details of the operation and to explore options for how it could be sold if needed. He wanted to know any areas of concern or faults I could find.

I felt what he *really* wanted me to tell him was that the safety risks were too great and he should sell the aircraft and rely on private operators. I could see the genuine concern on his face as he briefed me.

Our perspectives are the way we choose to see and interpret a situation. They're the lens through which we perceive events, other people and ourselves in relation to a challenging problem. The perspectives we choose are shaped by our experiences, emotions, values and expectations; a vast database within, from which our minds draw. The perspectives we adopt about a situation feel instinctive, because they are sourced from our subconscious mind and operate outside of our awareness unless we examine them.

I have no doubt my client was unaware of his default perspective on the problem and how it was influencing those around him. He was responding to an emotional fear of a situation he had no prior experience dealing with. He wanted this feeling to be gone, preferably by removing the aircraft operations from his business.

In the end I advised him to retain the aircraft capability as it was operated by highly skilled and trained personnel at standards at or above large-scale commercial operators. It was also commercially the most advantageous solution to the problem of transporting crew to remote locations. My 'perspective' was accepted only after addressing all the fear-based concerns he held that were influenced by his perspective of the problem at the outset.

Perspective always precedes action. It orientates us to act. If we perceive a situation as dangerous, we will act with abundant caution. If we perceive a situation as a great opportunity, we will act with purpose and curiosity.

Perspectives are generally lightly held and can be influenced with greater awareness. A small shift in perspective can have a significant impact. Where you typically think of only threats and fear, by shifting to think with curiosity you will start to see possibilities. Where you typically focus on finding faults, if you shift to look to leverage strengths, you'll start to find opportunities that were hidden from view. A shift in perspective can help you discover what you otherwise wouldn't have found.

Perspective IQ framework

Gaining awareness of your default problem-solving perspectives is made easier when you have a frame of reference to work with. It provides a context for reflection, helping uncover aspects of your thinking and actions you have previously been unaware of. Carl Jung said, "Until you make the unconscious conscious, it will direct your life, and you will call it fate". Cultivating self-awareness of your perspectives towards problems gives you the power to change them.

I had always viewed problems as obstacles; as thorns to be removed or avoided. It was a habit I developed as a child and reinforced in the work I chose to do. I never gave this perspective much thought until a client years ago said something that shifted my thinking. They said, "You've now told me all the problems I need to worry about and how to deal with them, but what about the problems I can get excited about and use to drive this business forward?" This exchange shifted my thinking about every problem I now see. Look for the downside as well as the upside and find a path to maximise how to deal with both sides.

Our perspective on problems influences how we approach them, how creative we are in finding solutions, and whether we give up or persevere when we experience difficulties. A perspective that views problems as threats, for example, will lead to fear, stress and anxiety, while a perspective that sees problems as opportunities for growth fosters resilience and creativity. How we choose to see things is a form of intelligence that can be developed.

> **Your perspective always precedes your actions.**

When I went searching for a tool to help better understand my own problem-solving perspectives, I couldn't find one that was simple and worked easily for me. So I developed my own. I call it the Perspective IQ framework.

The Perspective IQ framework aims to help you better understand your default problem-solving perspectives, how they serve you and where changes can improve the outcomes you achieve. Using it will give you more conscious flexibility to choose your responses and be less unconsciously reactive when facing a problem.

The Perspective IQ framework consists of nine contrasting problem-solving perspectives grouped across three dimensions. Each of the nine contrasting perspectives includes a description, along with a list of its strengths and limitations. These will help you identify what you typically focus on more and what you may overlook or dismiss – and the implications of doing this. With this insight, you can then decide if shifting your perspective in some areas would help improve how you approach and solve problems.

Perspective IQ dimensions

1. **Personal:** How we see ourselves in relation to problems. It reflects what we typically feel most comfortable with when we are facing them.
2. **Situational:** What we view problems as typically needing from us. It reflects how we see problems are best solved.
3. **External:** How we see problems from the perspective of others. It reflects how we typically choose to see and work with people to solve them.

PERSPECTIVE IQ FRAMEWORK		
Personal perspective		
When approaching problems are you typically more:		
Opportunity focused	or	Obstacle focused
Perfectionist	or	Pragmatist
Reflective	or	Action-oriented
Situational perspective		
When approaching problems are you typically more:		
Analytical	or	Intuitive
Cautious	or	Curious
Scarcity focused	or	Abundance focused
External perspective		
When approaching problems are you typically more:		
Controlling	or	Trusting
Collaborative	or	Independent
Fault finding	or	Strength finding

Personal perspective

Opportunity vs obstacle

Opportunity bias

Those with an opportunity bias view problems as openings for growth, learning or advancement. They tend to see difficulties as stepping stones rather than barriers, which allows them to approach problems with optimism. This proactive outlook often leads to resilience, as people with this perspective are motivated to find value in both the process and the outcome of problem-solving.

The strength of this perspective lies in its capacity for seeing the good and positive in what is presented. It fosters resourcefulness, allowing people to use challenges as springboards for creating something better. However, it can also lead to excessive risk-taking or ignoring credible downsides, as their focus may shift too heavily towards future possibilities rather than addressing present issues.

Obstacle bias

Those with an obstacle bias focus more on the barriers and difficulties of a problem. They see something that needs to be removed more than what can be created.

The strength of this perspective is in its surgical view of a potential problem. However, it can be limiting if it results in excessive focus on the negative aspects, preventing creative or innovative solutions.

Example

A leader with a stronger opportunity perspective might view market disruptions as a chance to pivot and innovate a business strategy. While a leader with a stronger obstacle perspective might focus more on mitigating the market disruption through defensive and loss minimisation strategies.

Perfectionist vs pragmatist

Perfectionist bias

Those with a perfectionist bias strive for the best possible outcome, prioritising focusing on finding the ideal solution to a problem. They enjoy the satisfaction of creating something they consider impressive. This meticulous attention to detail ensures high-quality results, but it can also lead to decision-making paralysis or delays if the perfect solution isn't readily attainable. Imperfection feels like failure for people with a perfectionist bias.

The strength of this perspective is in its pursuit of excellence, ensuring that problems are solved thoroughly and precisely. However, it can lead to frustration or inefficiency when perfection is not practical or not needed to solve a problem.

Pragmatist bias

Those with a pragmatist bias focus on workable solutions that are 'good enough' for the situation at hand. They prioritise efficiency and practicality, understanding that the perfect solution may not always be necessary or available. People with this bias like quick decisions and value their time above perfection. They are grounded and practical in their thinking, and less influenced by the opinions of others than they are by their opinion of themselves.

The strength of this perspective lies in its adaptability and ability to move challenges forward, even in less-than-ideal circumstances. However, it can sometimes lead to overlooking longer-term consequences or deeper issues, as the focus predominantly is on short-term results.

Example

A perfectionist software developer might delay launching an app until every bug is fixed preferring to prioritise positive market feedback over speed. A pragmatic developer would prefer to release a functional version and plan to improve it over time through updates, minimising the risk of negative market feedback over speed to market.

Reflective vs action-oriented

Reflective bias

Those with a reflective bias focus on thoughtful strategy, prioritising deep analysis and a deep understanding of the situation before acting. They excel at evaluating the complexities of a problem, weighing potential outcomes, and making decisions that are well-considered and geared towards long-term success.

This perspective is particularly strong in crafting strategic solutions that take into account broader implications, without being overly distracted by short-term challenges. However, it can sometimes lead to overthinking or delays when swift decisions are necessary.

Action-oriented bias

Those with an action-oriented bias value decisiveness and are eager to create momentum. They prefer to jump into action, learning as they go, and are comfortable adjusting their course along the way. They don't fear failure as much as they fear standing still and not making progress.

The strength of this perspective is its ability to create and maintain progress and adapt to changes in real time. However, it can sometimes lead to hasty decisions or overlooking or dismissing important details.

Example

A reflective manager might take time to research the best approach to solve a problem with long-term benefits, while an action-oriented manager might implement a temporary solution and refine it over time.

Situational perspective

Analytical vs intuitive

Analytical bias

Those with an analytical bias prefer breaking down problems into smaller components, relying on data, facts and evidence to guide decision-making. This systematic approach often leads to thorough, well-considered solutions that minimise risks.

The strength of this perspective is in its rigour and ability to create data-backed, methodical decisions. However, it can sometimes be too slow or rigid, as over-analysis may delay action, especially when rapid decisions are needed.

Intuitive bias

Those with an intuitive bias value instinct and experience over extensive data collection. They often make quicker decisions based on gut feelings or prior knowledge, which can be highly effective in dynamic or uncertain environments.

The strength of this perspective is its agility and flexibility, allowing for swift decision-making without being bogged down by excessive details. However, it may lead to errors if important data or information are overlooked, and safeguards are not put in place to manage common cognitive traps.

Example

A marketing specialist with a stronger analytical perspective may prefer to conduct extensive research before launching a new product. A similar marketing specialist with a stronger intuitive perspective may prefer to launch based on an instinctive sense that the product will resonate well with the target audience. Both approaches have their place, depending on the context and demands of the market.

Cautious vs curious

Cautious bias

Those with a cautious bias concentrate on risk minimisation, ensuring that every action is carefully planned and all potential pitfalls are considered before moving forward. They prioritise double-checking information and avoiding reckless decisions, which results in safer, well-informed choices that reduce the likelihood of failure.

The strength of this perspective is excelling at preventing mistakes and guarding against unnecessary risks, but it may lead to hesitation and missed opportunities when more innovative, high-reward actions are required. Excessive caution can also make it difficult to seize high-potential possibilities due to their associated risks.

Curious bias

Those with a curious bias thrive on exploration and discovery, viewing problems as opportunities to learn and experiment. They are more likely to explore untested methods and creative approaches to problem-solving, which can lead to groundbreaking solutions and highly valuable results.

The strength of this perspective is its openness to new ideas and adaptability in unfamiliar situations. However, it can also result in unnecessary risk-taking or pursuing too many ideas at once without proper focus.

Example

A cautious engineer might choose a reliable but outdated method for solving a technical issue. While a curious engineer might experiment with a cutting-edge solution that carries both risk and potential breakthroughs.

Scarcity vs abundance

Scarcity bias

Those with a scarcity bias believe resources, opportunities and success are limited. This often leads to a focus on preserving what they already have and avoiding risks they are unfamiliar with managing. They are quick to raise defences in the face of perceived threats or unfamiliar situations.

The strength of this perspective is in its practicality and ability to prevent overextension or unnecessary risk. However, it can also unknowingly limit innovation, as they may be too focused on protecting current resources rather than exploring new opportunities.

Abundance bias

Those with an abundance bias operate in the belief that there are plenty of resources and opportunities to go around. They often think where one door closes, another will open. They are more relaxed with ambiguity and uncertainty, believing solutions will be found to even the most challenging problems. People with this perspective are more likely to embrace risk-taking and collaboration, as they don't view success as a zero-sum game.

The strength of this perspective is its openness to new ideas and optimistic, expansive thinking. However, it can also result in overconfidence, lack of urgency, or taking on too much without sufficient resources to back it up.

Example

A scarcity-minded leader may hesitate to share information with potential partners, fearing they will lose their competitive advantage, while an abundance-minded leader would embrace collaboration, believing that sharing ideas will lead to greater mutual success.

External perspective

Controlling vs trusting

Controlling bias

Those with a controlling bias view close management and oversight as essential for success. They often feel they need to maintain direct control over all aspects of solving a problem to ensure everything goes as planned and aligns with their view of what success looks like. It provides them with a sense of security and reduces their fear of failure by prioritising precision and thoroughness in execution.

The strength of this perspective lies in its attention to detail and ability to mitigate risks through careful monitoring and applying judicious intervention. However, it can also lead to micromanagement, which can stifle creativity and hinder collaboration and development in others.

Trusting bias

Those with a trusting bias prioritise delegating responsibility and allowing others to take ownership of tasks. They trust their team members to carry out their duties competently, focusing on the bigger picture rather than every small detail. They focus on hiring and choosing the best team to give them confidence.

The strength of this perspective is its ability to foster collaboration, creativity, and empowerment, as individuals feel trusted and valued. However, it carries the risk that without enough oversight, critical details may be missed, or tasks may not be completed to the desired standard, compromising results.

Example

A controlling manager might insist on reviewing every aspect of a project to ensure it meets their standards, potentially delaying progress. In contrast, a trusting manager would delegate tasks and trust their team to execute them effectively, creating a more collaborative and faster-moving environment.

Collaborative vs independent

Collaborative bias

Those with a collaborative bias believe working together as a team not only leads to better results, it's also a much more enjoyable way of spending time. They enjoy being with people. They value diverse input, actively seek feedback, and thrive in environments where ideas are shared openly. Collaborative people encourage brainstorming, debate, and co-creation, leading to solutions that consider multiple viewpoints.

The strength of this perspective is that it often results in well-rounded, innovative solutions that benefit from collective intelligence. However, it may also slow down progress and decision-making, as coordinating with others and reaching a consensus can take more time than with a more direct approach.

Independent bias

Those with an independent bias prefer to work alone or with very few people, valuing autonomy and self-reliance. They believe they can achieve better results without the distractions or compromises that often come with group dynamics. It is efficient for quick decision-making and is especially effective when deep focus or individual expertise is required.

The strength of this perspective lies in its speed and self-sufficiency, but it can also limit the scope of solutions, as it can overlook insights that come from collaboration.

Example

A person with a collaborative bias might lead a group meeting to solve a complex issue, drawing on the diverse experiences of the team to create a comprehensive solution. Whereas a person with an independent bias, may prefer to tackle the same problem alone, relying on their expertise to find a fast and focused solution.

Fault finding vs strength finding

Fault-finding bias

Those with a fault-finding bias tend to focus on identifying weaknesses, mistakes and areas where improvement is needed. It can be very useful for refining processes, learning from errors, and ensuring that the root causes of problems are addressed.

The strength of this perspective is its ability to highlight flaws and prevent them from becoming larger issues. However, an excessive focus on faults may lead to a negative mindset and culture within a team, where shortcomings dominate thinking, stifling creativity and momentum.

Strengths bias

Those with a strength finding bias emphasise recognising and capitalising on what is already working well. People with this focus concentrate on leveraging their own and others' capabilities to overcome challenges, preferring to see problems as opportunities to use strengths strategically.

The strength of this approach is its positivity and resourcefulness, which fosters confidence and motivation. However, it can sometimes overlook critical weaknesses that need to be addressed, leading to over-reliance on strengths that may not be sufficient in all situations.

Example

A manager with a fault-finding bias might overly focus a team meeting on identifying errors made, aiming to eliminate them from occurring in the future. A manager with a strength-finding bias, however, would spend more time highlighting what the team did well and encourage building on those successes to improve performance further to overcome past underperformance.

How to use the Perspective IQ framework

Understanding your default perspectives on problem-solving gives you the flexibility to adapt your thinking to each specific problem. It also enables you to adjust or counteract these perspectives where they could hinder your progress. Where there's too much fault finding, for example, you will likely prioritise looking for what's wrong and not spend enough time on what's right. It's about finding the balance of perspectives that best fits the problem you need to solve. The more aware you are of your perspectives, the greater your capacity to adapt.

To uncover your default problem-solving perspectives, follow these steps:

1. **IDENTIFY YOUR CURRENT BIAS**
   The first step is to determine where you currently stand on each of the nine perspective preferences. Using a total score of 10, allocate the strength of your bias across each perspective. For example, for the opportunity vs obstacle perspective, if you typically see problems more as opportunities than obstacles you might score Opportunity focus as eight and Obstacle focus as two. Repeat this across all nine perspectives.

2. **EXAMINE POTENTIAL BLIND SPOTS**
   For scores less than three, consider the reasons why you choose to not hold this perspective often and whether there would be value in adopting a more balanced perspective in future. For someone with a strong opportunity bias, the obstacle perspective may initially seem overly negative. But by understanding the value of recognising barriers and limitations, you can start to adopt a more balanced view that appreciates both the potential of an opportunity and the realistic challenges that must be addressed.

3. PRACTICE USING THE OPPOSING PERSPECTIVE

To develop a more adaptive problem-solving approach, practice consciously using the opposing perspective. For example, if you have a strong abundance perspective and frequently assume there will always be time to find solutions, try to adopt a scarcity mindset for certain situations to ensure you're not overly relying on unproven assumptions.

CHAPTER 4

Perspective Intelligence

- Understanding your problem-solving perspectives brings awareness to the biases, habits, and preferences that shape how you approach them.
- With awareness of your perspectives, you can recognise blind spots or biases that distort your judgement, helping you make more balanced and objective decisions.
- Knowing your natural tendencies allows you to shift between different problem-solving strategies depending on what's most useful.
- Awareness of your own perspectives also enables you to understand and appreciate the perspectives of others, which can strengthen teamwork, and communication in group problem-solving.
- By seeing how your perspective influences outcomes, you gain insights that can help you refine your approach over time, becoming more effective and versatile in tackling future problems.

CHAPTER 5

Failure is just feedback

"Failure should be our teacher, not our undertaker. Failure is delay, not defeat. It is a temporary detour, not a dead end."
Denis Waitley

When we work on challenging problems, some things will go as we expect, and others will not. Failure, therefore, is to be expected. However, I believe we've been looking at failure all wrong. We are conditioned to think failure is bad. Schools use grading systems to judge how well we have learned what we've been taught from age six. We get used to a 'pass' as being good and worthy of praise, and a 'fail' as being bad and resulting in shame. As we progress further in the education system, the pressure to perform becomes stronger and the perceived consequences of failure as more significant to our lives.

First entering the workforce, we can carry with us at least 15 years of conditioning, from early schooling and university, that failure is viewed as something to avoid. So it's not surprising that this colours our perception of failure when we see it in others or experience it ourselves in the workplace. It can cause unnecessary fear and stifles creativity and innovation if we see failure as something to always avoid.

Failure is just feedback; data that tells us something did not meet our expectations and encourages us to learn why. Some failures are unpleasant, costly and are best avoided, to be sure. Others can be good to have and, in the right doses, help us learn faster and achieve more. Anyone in a product development or other creative role will know there is no such thing as a perfect first version.

Author Ann Lamott in her book *Bird by Bird*, a writing guide for authors, says, "...the only way I can get anything written at all, is to write really, really shitty first drafts"[13]. She knew starting something that hadn't been done before meant experimentation, iteration and refinement.

A shitty first draft could be viewed as a failure because it wasn't perfect the first time. We could view it as making a mistake that we need to correct to get it right. But that's not how she saw it. And other writers I've spoken with say the same. It would stop them writing, they told me, if that's how they viewed mistakes and failure. Creating something new, which means solving problems that haven't been solved before, necessarily involves not meeting expectations all the time. And in the right context, that's okay.

> **Failure is just feedback. Data that's tell us something did not meet our expectations and encourages us to learn why.**

What causes us to feel bad about failure is influenced by what meaning we give it. If we hold on tightly to perfection or lack of failure as an important condition for us to feel safe and secure, then we will naturally do whatever it takes to avoid failure ourselves. With this perspective, we see failure as an unacceptable condition for us to survive.

Failure, or something not meeting our expectations, gives us a choice: whether to update our knowledge and skills or ignore it and keep believing what we've always believed, doing what we've always done. The second option is the ostrich strategy of burying your head in the sand and hoping things will magically go away or get better on their own.

Thomas Edison once said, "I've not failed 10,000 times. I've not failed once. I've succeeded in proving that those 10,000 ways won't work."

He knew deviations from his expectations were necessary to help create something that hadn't been created before. He had no roadmap for guaranteed success. Failure gave him feedback to find the path to success. Judging his failures negatively would have sapped him of the energy he needed to keep progressing.

Ray Dalio, founder of Bridgewater Associates, one of the world's largest hedge funds, sees mistakes as a puzzle to give him clues on how to get better and remember what he had learned[14]. "So, I made a lot of painful mistakes", Dalio said. "And with time, my attitude about those mistakes began to change. I began to think of them as puzzles, that if I could solve the puzzles, they would give me gems. The puzzles were what would I do differently in the future so I wouldn't make that painful mistake. And the gems were principles that I would write down so I would remember them, that would help me in the future."

My first art exhibition was part of a collective of 120 other artists called The Other Art Fair, hosted at the Cutaway in Barangaroo, Sydney; a cavernous, enclosed space with exposed sandstone walls on one side and the foundation brickwork to a newly created public park on the other. It's a stone's throw from Sydney Harbour and is a spectacular setting for artists to show their works. Over 10,000 members of the public attended across the four days of the show.

I spoke with over a thousand people and many more stopped by to take a closer look at my works. My fellow artist neighbours were all veterans of the art world and had developed a sales patter that informed, enticed and gently guided people to purchase their works. It was masterful to watch.

By five p.m. on Sunday, the last day of the exhibition, I had sold only a fraction of my displayed works. I fell well short of my target. My initial reaction was deflation and defeat. My perspective was being shaped by what I had lost, not what I had gained. When I noticed my reaction, I paused and said to myself, "Okay, so what did I gain from this? What did I learn and how valuable is that?"

As it was my first exhibition, I had to learn everything from scratch—most of it unseen to people who come to the show and buy the art that's on exhibition. I learned how to size and fit out an exhibition stand, how to pack the paintings and hang them quickly, what specialist insurances I needed to purchase, how to price my works, how to engage potential collectors and, most importantly, I learned what it took for dozens of other artists to create, finesse and market their works to an audience that truly appreciated what they did.

All these things I would not have learned if I didn't participate in the exhibition. Choosing to judge my participation as a failure because I didn't sell as many works as I had hoped would have made the entire experience seem negative. It would become another barrier to continue pursuing my passion for creating art that inspires and delights people. And it didn't seem smart to put more barriers in front of me when I was just starting out. The only real failure would have been for this one metric to stop my progress.

Failure comes in flavours

You might be saying to yourself, "My manager is all over me about not making mistakes in my work and tracks our 'success rates' for everything we do. We have targets to hit and if we don't, that's viewed as bad. So how can you say that failure isn't bad and it's just feedback?"

Good question!

There is merit in expecting the absence of mistakes, errors or failures in some parts of a business. But not in every part. Where there are routine activities that, if performed diligently, can produce reliable results, then with the proper training and conditions it's reasonable to expect a very low failure rate. There are also failures that have a very low probability of happening and are the result of a cascade of things that go wrong. And there are failures that are the result of experimentation and pursuing what is uncertain.

There is a more refined way of looking at failure that can accommodate it as both necessary *and* avoidable. Harvard professor

Amy Edmondson has studied failure closely. Through her research, she found there are three different types of failures.

1. **Preventable failures**: deviations from outcomes we expect that are controllable. These are usually in well-defined and repeatable processes where almost all variables can be predicted and managed. Administrative or production processes are good examples of where failures are not desirable or expected where proper training, tools and conditions are provided.
2. **Unavoidable failures**: which arise from unique combinations of problems in complex systems. These include environments such as triaging patients in an emergency department, sending astronauts into space, or driving in a Formula 1 car race. Failures in these environments aren't always controllable and are guarded against by having multiple redundancy systems and a readiness to respond.
3. **Intelligent failures**: are when we are creating something new, innovating a product or service and provide valuable information to enable progress. It's the domain of solving challenging problems. There is much less control over these failures and usually a high likelihood there will be deviations from expectations. Learning from these failures is essential to innovation and progress.

When solving problems, there will always be uncertainty. The degree of uncertainty is dependent on the type of problem you're trying to solve. If your problem has been solved many times before, and there's a playbook on how to solve it, then you can expect that failure could be viewed negatively if it occurs.

However, even in this circumstance, where a team collaborates to solve a problem and where one or more people have not solved it before, there will be some risk of failure, because they will be learning. Doing something for the first time means there will be testing and learning to get it right.

For problems that don't have a ready playbook of solutions, you should expect some failures to help guide your progress. To think otherwise is unrealistic. It is limiting to you because you'll put unrealistic pressure on yourself to be perfect, and when you aren't (which is highly likely) you'll just give yourself unnecessary grief and stress which will impact how you feel and how you perform.

It's also limiting to others working with you, because they will feel the fear of failure and this limits the energy, creativity and focus they can put towards solving the problem, which makes it harder for them to perform at their best. Even the word 'failure' should be used cautiously. It's a word of judgement that can invoke emotional pain. Rather than focus on what you didn't achieve, focus on what has been achieved and after that, the gap to where you want to be. Failure highlights a gap, a difference, a confirmation of what doesn't work, a door that has closed for another to be opened and, above all, an opportunity to learn.

Treat success and failure with the same calmness

One of the world's greatest tennis players, Roger Federer, played 1,536 matches in his professional career and won almost 80% of them. But of all the points he played, he won 54% and lost 46%. Reflecting on his career, he said, "When you lose almost every second point you learn not to dwell on every shot. When you're playing a point, it must be the most important thing in the world. When it's behind you, it's behind you. This mindset is really crucial because it frees you to fully commit to the next point and the point after that."

Negative energy is wasted energy, he believes. "You want to become a master at overcoming hard moments. That to me is the sign of a champion."[15]

If you rely too much on the highs of success, you will equally be drawn into the abyss of the lows that inevitably accompany striving to solve problems that challenge you. This repeated cycle of chasing highs and feeling crushing lows when you fail to realise your expectations will act as a handbrake on your ability to take further risks, because you will eventually want to avoid feeling the lows of necessary failure on the path to success. The antidote is to accept failure as part of success and learn to quickly let go of negative feelings that can accompany them.

When failure triggers grief

To feel disappointment from failure is normal. Where failure turns into overwhelming feelings of loss, we need more than a shift in perspective to help us manage the feelings of grief that accompany it. No one likes experiencing significant failure. Failure can feel like a deep loss where you have a strong emotional attachment to a future outcome that doesn't materialise as you hoped it would. We all have hopes and expectations, and the tighter we hold onto these, the more we feel loss and grief when what we hope for is 'taken' from us. When we experience an intense emotional loss, our mind and body shift into a state of grief. It's a survival mechanism to process the emotions of loss and enable healing.

Renowned grief expert David Kessler defines experiencing grief as, "... a change you didn't want to have". It encompasses a range of feelings, including sadness, anger, guilt and confusion. It can cause a range of physical symptoms, including loss of sleep, decreased motivation, reduced energy levels, and heightened nervous system reactivity.

When solving challenging problems, we can put both what *we have* and what *we hope to have* at risk of loss. Experiencing failure that causes either type of loss can feel extremely painful. The depth of this pain is proportionate to the level of emotional investment and meaning we give to the loss. In short, where we experience failure that has significant emotional meaning, it becomes a loss that we may need to grieve.

Elisabeth Kübler-Ross identified five stages of grief and loss in 1969. In 2019, Kessler added a sixth stage of grief in his book *Finding Meaning*.

The six stages of grief are:

1. **Denial**: shock and disbelief that the loss has occurred.
2. **Anger**: that what we had or hoped for is no longer available to us.
3. **Bargaining**: all the what ifs and regrets.
4. **Depression**: sadness and emotional pain from the loss.
5. **Acceptance**: acknowledging the reality of the loss.
6. **Meaning**: understanding and making sense of the loss and letting it go.

You may have heard the saying, "When bad things happen, find a way to turn lemons into lemonade". What it means is find a way to create a positive out of the negative and it will set you free of the bitter taste of defeat. What it doesn't tell you is if you've been served a truck load of lemons, you first need to get yourself properly prepared to create lemonade. For that, we need to pass through the six stages of grief and let the feelings of loss attached to it go.

The point of grieving is to set us free from the pain of loss. Kessler says, "Healing doesn't mean that loss didn't happen. It means that it no longer controls us". Where we stay stuck in anger or bargaining, for example, it controls how we think and act. And that makes getting back to work and pursuing problems that will help you grow much harder. It affects your judgement, decision-making, motivation, and interactions with others.

Passing through grief takes time and patience. The extent of the failure and attached feelings of loss will determine the time it takes to bounce back. Be patient with yourself if you need to process grief. If you've suffered multiple failures in succession, grief can take hold as a way of processing the cumulative effect of these losses.

A piece of advice that Kessler has in his book *Meaning* profoundly shaped how I approach grief and has helped me enormously. Kessler says *we need to have our grief witnessed without judgement by others to fully recover from loss.* What he found was that people who stayed stuck in their grief hadn't found a way to share how it made them feel with someone they trusted fully and completely.

Before learning this, I believed I just needed to tough it out and rationalise grief. It was the last thing on my to-do list to share it with someone else in a vulnerable way. But having now learned how to process the grief of significant failure and loss, it has made me far more confident to take more risk and pursue larger challenges. Feelings of grief are only temporary and will pass.

Bearing witness means sharing your experience with a colleague, loved one, friend or mentor. The important thing is to be completely honest with what happened and how the failure and loss made you feel, and the reason it's so significant to you. There is no need for solutions or lessons learned in this moment. Just to let out what has been held inside without fear of judgement. This process will help you let go of the negative feelings associated with failure and allow you to learn and recover to take on new challenges faster.

CHAPTER 5

Failure is just feedback

- Failure is a just an event where our expectations were not met. It's feedback for us to interpret and learn from.
- Identify the type of failure: preventable, unavoidable or intelligent, to guide how you plan for and respond to it.
- Failure presents a choice: to learn and adapt or remain unchanged and stuck in old patterns.
- Treat failures as puzzles to spark curiosity, which drives learning and progress.
- When the scale of a failure becomes emotionally overwhelming, progress through the six stages of grief to finding meaning in the experience to let it go.

A Problem Hunter's Mindset

OVERVIEW

Mindset encompasses the ingrained attitudes, beliefs and thought patterns that dictate how we behave. Heavily influenced by our subconscious, our mindset acts as a habitual framework that guides our thoughts and actions. Mindset is vital in problem-solving because it shapes how we approach challenges, interpret situations and make judgements. It works in concert with our perspective. But unlike perspective, which can shift based on the specific situation, mindset—particularly core beliefs—tends to be enduring and apply consistently because it forms the basis of our identity. What we believe, we become.

In this section, we explore how mindset, beliefs, our inner critical voice and common thinking traps shape how we approach and solve problems. They can influence us to see them as springboards to become inspiring leaders. They can also unconsciously limit our thinking, choices and actions, making efforts to solve problems much harder than it needs to be.

When we become aware of limiting beliefs, critical inner voice and thinking traps that operate in our minds, we have the power to shift and tame them, which gives us greater freedom to pursue challenging problems that create opportunity. Awareness allows us to replace self-doubt with self-confidence and empowers us to create a mindset aligned with growth, possibility and purpose. It sets the foundation to become a problem hunter.

CHAPTER 6

Problems create leaders

"It always seems impossible until it's done."
Nelson Mandela

Unexpected problems create opportunities for anyone to become an inspiring leader. A phone call at one a.m. on a Saturday morning pierced the silence at Rosalie and Gareth Akerman's home in KwaZulu-Natal, South Africa. Gareth picked up his phone and in a crackled voice said, "Hello, its Gareth who is calling please?"

An anxious voice responded, "Hello Gareth, I'm sorry to inform you sir, but I believe your factory has caught fire and is ablaze". The husband and wife team, who had spent the past four years pouring their hearts and souls into building their dream business—one that did genuine good for the environment, the community and their family—leaped out of bed, hearts and minds racing. They bundled up their two young children and dashed out the front door to start what would be the most challenging and rewarding problem-solving exercise of their lives.

A few days before the fire, there was a break-in at the local electrical substation, located a short distance from the factory. Rosalie had called the local municipality and informed them about the break-in so they could come and inspect the property to see if everything was okay. After that, she thought nothing more about it. Unknown to them at the time, thieves had stolen a one-metre length of copper cable from the substation.

On Friday, the day before the fire, Rosalie and Gareth cancelled the night shift and told their staff to finish early. They had achieved record production for the month and had a warehouse full of pre-ordered stock. Their spirits were high, and they wanted everyone to enjoy the weekend. This was just three days after the break-in at the electrical substation.

That evening, a large storm passed over the factory. A lightning bolt hit the metal roof. Normally the energy from a lightning strike would be discharged through a copper earth cable. This time the surge in electricity caused the large cables running in the factory roof to 'flare'. The one-metre length of copper cable, stolen from the electricity substation, was no longer providing the safety of an earth cable to protect the factory.

> **Unexpected problems create opportunities for anyone to become an inspiring leader.**

Sparks from the electricity cables ignited the wood and insulation in the roof. A fire quickly spread and engulfed the building. It destroyed all their stock and manufacturing equipment. Thirty people would have been working in the factory at the time of the fire had they not cancelled the night shift the day before.

Rosalie and Gareth's business was created to do good. At the time of the fire, their business took 6,000 tonnes of industrial rubber waste products destined for landfill each year and recycled them into usable rubber raw materials they sold to local and international tire retread, conveyor belt and artificial turf manufacturers.

They employed 70 local workers who relied on their jobs to lift them out of poverty. They had a loyal group of suppliers and customers committed to supporting them because of the good they were doing for the environment and the quality of their products. It took weeks for firefighters to extinguish the blaze. Nothing was salvageable.

Rosalie and Gareth had insurance that covered the costs of relocating the factory and purchasing new equipment. However, the odds are stacked against a successful restart for any business after a disaster. Forty percent of businesses don't reopen, and of the ones that do, 25% fail within one year and 90% fail within two years.[16]

To start again, Rosalie said, "We need a way to keep everyone focused on positive rather than negative thoughts about what had just happened and the work that needs to be done". This new problem provided an opportunity to lead in a different way; a way that embraced fear, sorrow, loss and suffering and healed them through purpose and gratitude.

She wondered, "What if we make it a core value that when something bad happens, we will do something good in equal proportion? No matter how big or small."

Studies have shown the brain can't respond to anxiety and gratitude at the same time, which means it's one or the other. We can feel anxious and other negative states, or we can feel grateful and positive emotions. Rosalie and Gareth replaced despair with meaning and shifted their thoughts and conversations from fear to purposeful action.

They became aware of a problem within their community: abuse towards school-age children after they finished their school day. Looking into the problem, they learned most abuse occurred between the time children returned home from school and the time their parents or caregivers returned home after work. They decided this would become their focus—to create a safe space for children within their community after they finished school for the day.

A factory canteen was converted into a child-friendly space and an outside car park transformed into a play area with swings and a netball hoop. They partnered with a local charity to run the Safe Space program every weekday afternoon. Children were fed a healthy meal, supported with their homework, had a safe space to play and had access to a social worker if they needed it. Seventy children, ranging in ages between four and 17, used the space every day.

Seeing how much good their Safe Space project was providing children in their community created an overwhelming sense of daily pride and gratitude for Rosalie and Gareth and their staff. Helping to solve an important community problem helped dampen the anxiety and worry about recovering their business.

They also found another ingenious way to let go of worry each day. Rosalie placed a 'worry tree' at the top of her garden stairs. Inspired by Edward de Bono's 'six thinking hats' idea, she and her family visualised taking their worry hats off when they got to the top of the stairs and mentally hung them on the worry tree so they could walk into their home and be fully present with each other.[17]

The tree Rosalie chose was a native weeping boer-bean. It has tight clusters of red flowers and an abundance of dripping nectar. In the morning, they would collect their hanging worries from the worry tree on the way down the stairs. The worry tree helped shelter them from their worries each night, allowing them to rest and recover.

A year after the fire, Rosalie and Gareth opened their new rubber recycling factory. Their customers returned and suppliers provided stock on longer credit terms to help get them back on their feet, inspired by the leadership they had shown. The factory fire had provided an opportunity to develop Rosalie and Gareth into inspiring young leaders within their community.

Leaping at problems creates leadership roles

Leaders think of problems as mini trampolines that spring them forward. Jon Michail began his career as a young fashion designer for luxury brand Christian Dior. Working in his hometown of Melbourne, Jon loved the fashion business and had a flair for creating luxury menswear.

Jon's career leaped forward after he won the Australian Wool Corporation Young Designer of the year, lifting him from relative obscurity to design fame overnight. Eighteen months later, he left Christian Dior and founded premium menswear design and manufacturing business, Studio Jianni. His niche was creating luxury men's suits and business wear using premium fabrics imported from Italy, Germany, England and Switzerland.

Before he reached thirty, Jon, together with his wife and brothers, had grown his luxury menswear business to 200 staff and supplied major menswear fashion retailers across Australia. A large unpaid debt by one of his biggest retail customers triggered Jon to shift his focus to direct retail, vertically integrating his business into design, manufacturing and direct retail. He chose to leap at the opportunity to take over the retail lease of a customer that had failed to pay him. The move paid off. His direct retail footprint quickly grew to 10 stores in major fashion precincts and shopping malls across Melbourne.

As his retail presence grew, Jon noticed a pattern in his customers' behaviour. He found the men that came into his stores to buy new clothes struggled to understand how to create an image for themselves through their choices in clothing. His sales team was good at selling items of clothing, but not at curating an overall image that reflected what the customer wanted to project. He could see this was frustrating his customers and, as a result, it was hurting sales.

This observation gave Jon the idea of creating an image consulting business within his retail stores to cater for men who wanted bespoke support. His consulting service, he thought, would create an overall image for his customers through their clothing choices. The idea resonated and his image consulting business grew quickly, driving retail sales growth even faster.

As his image consulting clientele grew, Jon started spending more and more time supporting this fast-growing part of the business. He found he loved working with his clients, who would share their stories, aspirations and challenges with him. His clients would open up about their lives and ask for advice on more than just what clothes to wear. They were seeking life, career and business advice as well as image advice. He noticed his best clients, valued this the most. And it led him to his next business idea: to create a dedicated image consulting and personal branding business, separate from his fashion business.

Jon established Image Group International, a consulting business focused on personal branding, image consulting and reputation management. Jon's ambition was to combine "...the power of gravitas, the power of branding and positioning and the power of presence and looking good". His business has supported over 7,500 clients to link mind, body and spirit into their personal brand and reputation, including two former Australian prime ministers, CEOs of multinational businesses, heads of major consulting firms and leaders in the medical and legal professions. The business now has operations in 16 countries.

Jon leaped at the problems he saw in front of him and created a leadership role for himself where one previously didn't exist. He used each problem as an opportunity to create leadership roles that inspired him. The belief that problems create opportunities propelled him forward.

Solving your problem invites you to create a path to solve it for others

Rachel Drew founded Cadence in Saskatchewan, Canada to make the administration of deceased estates easier and more compassionate for the loved ones left behind who need to navigate it. Rachel is a thoughtful, empathic and determined Canadian—a set of qualities within the people who call Canada home that I came to greatly admire when I lived there.

The idea for Cadence came about when Rachel needed to navigate the paperwork and deal with lawyers, banks, government departments and myriad other parties to settle the estate of her late mother.

"This was a very intense time of my life. I had two kids under three years old and my husband was struggling with addiction at the time, and I was running a business that provided for us financially. After losing my mum, I quickly discovered the challenges of settling an estate. It is fragmented, stressful and time-consuming, and it occurs when people are least able to cope. I wanted to bring something into the world that could help people be in a better position than I was when I lost my mum."

She realised it wasn't a legal problem she had to solve; it was a complicated administrative problem that could be made so much easier for people. Rachel saw this problem as her opportunity to create a path to turn her pain into purpose to benefit many thousands of people.

CHAPTER 6

Problems create leaders

- Challenging problems provide the conditions that create inspiring leaders.
- Problems act as springboards that create leadership pathways that may otherwise wouldn't be available.
- How we solve a problem for ourselves provides the opportunity for us to solve it for others and create new leadership roles for ourselves.

CHAPTER 7

Turd observing stinks

"Don't find fault, find a remedy, anybody can complain."
Anonymous

During a conversation with Andrew Henry, the CFO of a large Australian infrastructure services business at the time, I asked him what frustrated him most about the people who worked in his team. He told me it was people who were fantastic at pointing out and describing problems but didn't show initiative or take responsibility for solving them.

These people, he said, "Were great at describing a pile of shit, pointing at it and getting others to stare at it too, but not doing the work of cleaning it up". You may know someone who's like this: quick to point out problems but never as quick to take action to solve them. I call this behaviour 'turd observing'. And it stinks!

Turd observing is not unusual in the workplace. In fact, it's so common it runs all the way up to the highest levels of an organisation, including in the United States Government. Giving career advice to young people, former US President Barack Obama said, "What I've seen at every level are people who are very good at describing problems. People who are very sophisticated in explaining why something went wrong or why something can't get fixed. But what I'm always looking for is, no matter how small or how big the problem is, somebody who says: 'let me take care of that'." [18]

Andrew Henry and President Obama both desperately wanted more people to work for them who would not only hunt for and describe problems in great detail, but also do the work to figure out how to solve them. In their eyes, these people were the most valuable to have in their organisation—people willing to find and solve challenging problems.

Problem-solving helps us develop new capabilities that protect and keep us safe. As we learned earlier, everything eventually will change and change creates new problems, which means we must find ways of solving them.

While we don't yet fully know how our brain works, what evolutionary history suggests is that our brains appear to be specifically designed to solve problems that help us survive. And we have evolved to solve problems while we are in unstable environments and in nearly constant motion.[19]

> **Problem-solving is the most in-demand set of skills globally**

The instability and uncertainty of our environment led our brains to be wired in an extremely flexible way to allow us to solve problems through exploration. To survive, we needed to learn through doing and making mistakes. We needed our brains to focus on and solve problems to learn and survive.

While many of the problems we face each day are relatively small, we will all face significant problems at some point in our careers and lives. We just don't know when. The more practice we get at solving problems, honing and developing our skills, the more confident and capable we become. And that means you'll be ready for whatever your workplace and life throw at you.

Solving problems that matter to us also gives us meaning. Finding meaning in our lives and in our work brings us satisfaction and peace. Viktor Frankl in his book *Man's Search for Meaning* argued that we ultimately find meaning in life by taking responsibility for finding solutions to the problems we are given and taking action to fulfil the tasks that bring these solutions to life.[20] Purpose and meaning are not discovered through excessive contemplation, he argued, but rather by taking focused action towards an outcome that is worthy of achieving.

Solving problems also supports our wellbeing. Research has shown that people who actively engage in problem-solving become better equipped to cope with stress, manage emotions and maintain overall wellbeing. By taking action to address challenges proactively, we reduce the negative impact of chronic stress on the body and mind, leading to improved physical health. Where we retain our skills and capacity to solve problems and maintain our independence as we age, we also live longer.[21]

For a business, problem-solving is an essential collective capability. A business exists to solve problems at scale. As a result, it needs a constant flow of new talent and upskilling of existing employees to cope with new and challenging problems that need to be solved. Problem-solving is the most in-demand set of skills globally.[22]

Problem-solving skills atrophy if we don't use them

Can we assume problem-solving skills will always be available when we need them? The short answer is no. Like all other skills we develop, they need to be practiced to be retained. It's the use-it-or-lose-it principle of how our minds work.

You may have become proficient in a second language at high school. Then, 10 years later, you travel overseas and want to use it. When you do, it feels rusty and awkward, and your vocabulary might only be 10% of what it once was. With practice, however, your skills return. But the key is that you need to practice skills to rediscover them.

What might shock you to learn is even essential hunting skills of apex predators can be 'forgotten' if not used. A study reported in *National Geographic* magazine found most large carnivores die if returned to their natural habitat after living too long in captivity, caused mainly by a lack of hunting skills.[23] That skill isn't needed while in captivity.

Even though it is a basic instinct, not practicing their hunting skills made it impossible for most of the animals released into the wild to survive.

Problem-solving for humans is like the hunting skills of wild animals. It's an essential survival skill. While much can be solved through technology and convenience services, these solutions are only ever temporary. To better prepare for a life that is more durable, independent and adaptable, we need to invest in developing and retaining our problem-solving skills. That means not just staring at problems. It means taking action to solve them.

CHAPTER 7

Turd observing stinks

- Spotting problems is useful, but finding remedies and taking action to solve them is far more valuable. It's what leaders want most from people who work for them.
- Problem-solving is the most in-demand set of skills globally.
- Practice your problem-solving skills or they will atrophy and weaken, like any other skill we learn.

CHAPTER 8

Beware your Judgement Junkie

"The most difficult times for many of us are the ones we give ourselves."
Tara Brach

We all have a potential Judgement Junkie lurking inside us. The Judgement Junkie is our critical inner voice that, left unchecked, can act like a constricting vine slowly wrapping around our potential, limiting our creative thinking and undermining our abilities to solve the problems we need and want to.

Judgement and critical thinking are some of the most powerful mechanisms our brain has for evaluating our environment and guiding and protecting our experiences. These cognitive processes, while valuable in many contexts, can become counterproductive when they dominate our thinking. The Judgement Junkie is our enemy within. The more you become aware of it, the greater your ability to tame and offset its impact on you. As Marcus Aurelius said, "Our life is what our thoughts make it".

Judgement is helpful, until it becomes limiting

Judgemental and critical thinking serve as fundamental mechanisms for navigating complex environments. From an evolutionary perspective, these tendencies were essential for survival. Tens of thousands of years ago, early humans relied on quick assessments and critical evaluations to discern threats, identify resources, and make decisions that ensured their wellbeing and safety. As such, the capacity for judgement and criticism is not inherently negative; rather, it's a tool that has evolved to help us navigate our environments effectively. It differs from our perspectives, which are the cognitive biases and preferences we have that shape how we see problems. Both are mental processes that combine to determine how we think about and take action to solve problems.

However, like a tool that can either build or destroy, judgemental and critical thinking must be used carefully and mindfully. Nowadays these tools are frequently overused, applied to situations where openness and flexibility would be more appropriate. We use our judgement excessively, and where it is overused, it can become negative if it's fed with limiting beliefs.

> **The Judgement Junkie is our enemy within. The more you become aware of it, the greater your ability to tame and offset its impact on you.**

My Judgement Junkie used to say to me when I was about to start something new, "You haven't done this before, and it looks hard, remember when you were let go you don't want that to happen again". I said this to myself all the time without realising it was a subconscious pattern. As a result, every time I started something new, I'd feel incredibly anxious. That's what our Judgement Junkie does. It can make life hard for us when it doesn't need to be.

Starting something new for me then felt harder because these thoughts took energy to counteract, took up brain capacity that I could have used to do the task, so it felt harder. It caused me to procrastinate when I faced doing difficult things.

The Judgement Junkie keeps us locked in defensive thinking, seeing negative when there is neutral or positive. Without realising it, if we listen too much to our Judgement Junkie, believe its interpretations of the world and fail to challenge them, we tend to act in ways that have negative consequences for us.

We develop our Judgement Junkie when we are young as a defence mechanism to cope with challenging and difficult situations where we feel threatened. It acts as a warning system, helping to anticipate and avoid situations that could lead to negative outcomes.

It may have been harsh words, unmet needs, altercations with others, or just being overwhelmed with a new situation we found unfamiliar. While its job is to create meaning and keep us safe, it does this by using critical and negative thoughts about ourselves and others to prevent us from being in similar situations again, even if we could cope well with them now.

The Judgement Junkie creates fear as an illusion to keep us safe

One of the most significant consequences of being overly judgemental and critical of ourselves is the development of high levels of fear and insecurity. When we constantly engage in self-criticism or judgemental thinking, we create a mental environment where fear and insecurity thrive.

This fear is most often irrational, rooted in the belief that any variation from perfection can result in catastrophic consequences. As a result, people become increasingly risk-averse, avoiding situations where they might fail or be judged. In my experience it's one of the most common reasons either problems go unaddressed or poor solutions are selected. Fear closes down humility and risk-taking—critical ingredients to solving problems. At an individual level it is stressful and career limiting. Scaled up to an organisational level it becomes a cancer-like problem.

Have you ever heard your critical inner voice say something like, "You can't afford to make any mistakes. If you fail, everyone will think you're incompetent. Better to stay quiet and not take any risks—it's safer that way"?

That's the Judgement Junkie.

The Judgement Junkie shuts down innovation and creativity

Innovation and creativity are essential to problem-solving. They involve generating new ideas, exploring novel solutions, and the willingness to challenge established norms. However, overly judgemental and critical thinking is inherently incompatible with the thinking required for these processes.

Innovation requires an open and flexible approach to thinking, where possibilities are explored without immediate judgement or criticism. In contrast, a judgemental and critical mindset is characterised by scepticism, caution and a preference for the familiar, all of which stifle the creative process.

The Judgement Junkie doesn't like ambiguity or uncertainty. It creates fear and discomfort to appear in control. Problems that are challenging and will create the most value for us and the organisation we work for will necessarily mean we need be comfortable being in a state of unknowing at times. Persisting through the discomfort of confusion and trial and error is where breakthroughs are made and innovative solutions are created.

Have you ever heard your critical inner voice say something like, "Your ideas are probably unrealistic and won't work. Better stick with what's already known and proven, or you'll just embarrass yourself and waste time"?

That's the Judgement Junkie.

The Judgement Junkie encourages us to jump to conclusions

People often jump to conclusions because it provides a sense of immediate certainty in situations where uncertainty or ambiguity might cause them discomfort. This is the work of the Judgement Junkie. Overly critical judgement narrows our perspective and prioritises fast evaluation over thoughtful analysis. It creates certainty when we feel uncomfortable not knowing what to do. We tend to focus on flaws and shortcomings, rather than what's interesting and possible, because that will cause us to linger in uncertainty for longer.

Quick decisions are helpful to create momentum and avoid unnecessary waste of time and resource, but when other options can and should be considered, it can severely limit how problems are understood and solved. It can also create a pervasive negative bias in how we perceive situations and people.

A bias to jump to conclusions conditions our minds to quickly assess information in a way that confirms our preconceived notions or fears. Instead of taking the time to gather all relevant information, consider alternative viewpoints, or seek deeper understanding, we leap to conclusions that align with our critical assessments.

The urge to quickly judge ourselves, situations and others often comes from a desire to protect ourselves from perceived threats or disappointments. By quickly identifying what we see as wrong or problematic, we try to regain a sense of control over our environment. Jumping to conclusions is a way to feel in control when we actually feel uncertain or out of control.

While it may feel good to make a decision or reach a conclusion fast, it often leads to errors in judgement, as we overlook important details, context or nuances that could change our understanding of a situation.

For example, if someone is overly critical of a colleague's work, they might quickly assume incompetence without considering factors such as workload, lack of resources, or personal challenges that could be affecting performance. This not only leads to unfair evaluations, but also damages relationships and limits a team's problem-solving capabilities.

Have you ever heard your critical inner voice say something like, "You already know what's wrong here. Don't waste time digging deeper. Just make the call and move on—there's no point in considering other possibilities"?

That's the Judgement Junkie.

The Judgement Junkie makes thinking overly rigid

Overly judgemental thinking creates highly rigid standards that we believe are inflexible. It leads to right or wrong thinking when the world is much more shades of grey.

Cognitive rigidity is when we can't adapt our thinking in response to new information or changing circumstances. This rigidity can manifest in various ways, such as clinging to preconceived notions, dismissing alternative viewpoints, or adhering strictly to established rules and procedures.

In problem-solving, cognitive rigidity is particularly detrimental as it limits the range of solutions considered, reduces the ability to adapt to complex and dynamic situations, and makes creating the best solutions to problems very hard to achieve.

Have you ever heard your critical inner voice say something like, "There's only one right way to handle this, and anything else is just wrong or a waste of time. Don't even bother considering other approaches"?

That's the Judgement Junkie.

The Judgement Junkie makes teamwork and collaboration harder

The Judgement Junkie can make relationships and our ability to collaborate much harder. Overly judgemental people create an environment of tension, defensiveness and mistrust. When people are quick to judge or criticise others, it creates a climate of fear and caution. When people feel there is a Judgement Junkie in a team they will become reluctant to express themselves or take risks. This creates blind spots and barriers for solving problems that are invisible to the naked eye.

My daughter is a wonderful dancer and competed in dance competitions in high school. She told me that to learn a dance well, and for it to look harmonious, both partners needed to feel comfortable and confident, free from the fear of missteps being harshly criticised. However, when one partner is overly judgemental, the other becomes hesitant, unsure of their footing, leading to a stiff and awkward interaction rather than a fluid and graceful movement.

It's the same feeling with the dance of establishing a team to work on problems that are hard and require experimentation and troubleshooting. As soon as overly judgemental comments or criticism start to flow, the barriers to cohesion and teamwork rise up.

To function effectively, teams rely on open communication, mutual respect and the free exchange of ideas. However, when people feel their contributions will be met with harsh criticism or judgement, they become hesitant to share their thoughts or propose new ideas. Twentieth century industrialist Charles Schwab, who was famous for his encouraging leadership style, said, "I have yet to find the person, however great or exalted his station, who did not do better work and put forth greater effort under a spirit of approval that he would ever do under a spirit of criticism".

This reluctance to openly share thoughts and ideas leads to a lack of diversity in perspectives and a reduction in the quality of creativity. At its worst, it can create a toxic work environment where people feel undervalued and disengaged, stifling problem-solving capacity and capability.

Have you ever heard your critical inner voice say something like, "If you share your idea, they'll just think it's stupid or criticise you for not thinking it through. It's safer to stay quiet and not say anything."?

That's the Judgement Junkie.

Taming the Judgement Junkie

If you're prone to negative and judgemental thinking like I am, take these steps to help tame your Judgement Junkie.

1. **ACKNOWLEDGE YOUR CRITICAL INNER VOICE**

    The first step to tame this limiting part of your mind is to become aware of it and to notice when your mind dives into a fear-based or critical narrative. Start by recognising when the critical inner voice is speaking.

    Pay attention to thoughts that are negative, judgemental or overly harsh assessments of your character or skills. Identify the specific messages or phrases it uses. Write them down to make them more concrete and easier to confront later.

2. **SEPARATE YOURSELF FROM THE JUDGEMENT JUNKIE**

    Treat the Judgement Junkie voice as an external entity rather than part of your identity. Imagine it as an outside critic, not an integral part of you. This helps reduce the emotional power it has over you. As Michael A Singer says, "You are not your thoughts".

3. **CHALLENGE AND REFRAME NEGATIVE THOUGHTS**

    Question the validity of the critical Judgement Junkie. Ask yourself if the thoughts are based on facts or assumptions.

    Reframe negative statements into more balanced, constructive ones. For example, change "I'm not good enough" to "I'm doing my best and I can improve with practice."

CHAPTER 8

Beware your Judgement Junkie

- We all have a potential Judgement Junkie, our critical inner voice, lurking inside us.
- An overly critical mindset is harmful because it closes the door to curiosity and prevents deeper understanding of problems and potential solutions.
- Tame your Judgement Junkie by acknowledging it exists and is separate from you, and challenge and reframe the negative thoughts you find get in the way of pursuing and solving challenging problems.

CHAPTER 9

Mindset Reset

"What lies behind us and what lies before us are tiny matters compared to what lies within us."
Ralph Waldo Emerson

What we believe about ourselves is who we become. What we believe about work and the world we live in directly influences how we approach challenges and interact with others, and ultimately shapes our experiences and the outcomes we achieve.

The beliefs people hold about themselves and what problems represent to them were the standout differences I found in my research on expert problem-solvers. People who ran towards problems and saw them as opportunities believed that was the path best for them to progress and develop. Their insecurities didn't overwhelm their belief in their capabilities. And because of this, they developed more experience and expertise faster than others who stood back.

They had either found ways to overcome limiting and harmful beliefs that had previously held them back or simply didn't have them, and found it curious why others struggled when they didn't. They had beliefs such as I am smart enough to work this out, I will be okay even if I fail, I am able to ask others for help, I know this will be good for my career and things that challenge me, make me stronger.

A belief is something we consider is true, real or exists, often without requiring evidence or proof. It is a mental representation or attitude that shapes how we interpret and understand the world around us.

Our beliefs are formed through experiences, cultural influences, education, and personal reflections.

Beliefs can be about anything, including:

1. **Facts or reality:** such as believing the earth is round or that gravity exists.
2. **Personal capabilities:** such as believing in your ability to succeed in a particular task or skill.
3. **Values and morals:** such as believing in the importance of honesty, integrity, openness and courage.

Beliefs can be empowering, motivating us to achieve goals and guiding us in making decisions that support our growth, or they can be limiting, holding us back by fostering fear, doubt or prejudice. They are deeply embedded in our mindset, but they are not fixed and can evolve with new experiences, information and perspectives. They can be changed.

Beliefs give us a reference point or a set of principles to rely on when making decisions. They help us make sense of the world by categorising and interpreting our experiences. For example, if you believe that hard work leads to success, you are more likely to make decisions that involve effort and persistence. If you believe comfort is more important than hard work, you will avoid challenging problems to work on.

> **A belief is something we consider is true, often without requiring evidence or proof.**

Our beliefs shape how we perceive and interpret information. They filter what we notice, how we evaluate options, and what we consider important. If you believe people are generally trustworthy, you are more likely to interpret others' actions positively and be open to collaboration. If you believe no one can be trusted and you should only truly rely on yourself, your ability to solve more complex problems that involve collaboration and input from others will be limited.

In uncertain situations, beliefs provide a sense of stability and predictability. They help reduce anxiety by offering clear guidelines or expectations. Believing in your ability to handle challenges can reduce fear and encourage taking action, even in uncertain or risky situations. If you believe feeling uncertain is painful and to be avoided, you will limit yourself to working on familiar and predictable problems, restricting your development.

Imagine working with someone who believed every problem has a solution if it's approached creatively and collaboratively. This belief would help shape how they acted in the face of problems in the following ways:

1. **Open-mindedness to solutions:** Because they believe in the power of creativity, they are likely to encourage brainstorming sessions where team members feel safe to share even unconventional ideas. This fosters an environment where innovation is valued, leading to a broader range of potential solutions being considered.
2. **Collaboration and inclusivity:** A belief in the benefits of collaboration means they would likely involve others in problem-solving, rather than trying to handle everything alone. This not only widens the diversity of ideas, but also builds team cohesion and buy-in to solutions.
3. **Resilience and persistence:** Holding a belief that every problem has a solution boosts resilience and persistence. When faced with setbacks or difficult problems as a result, they are less likely to give up. Instead, they view obstacles as challenges to be overcome, motivating themselves and others to keep searching for answers rather than feeling defeated.

What I found from my research is those people with more advanced problem-solving capabilities had more empowering beliefs than limiting beliefs.

It's normal and common to have beliefs that cause insecurities and undermine our performance at work. Seventy per cent of people experience impostor syndrome at some point in their lives, which is fed by negative beliefs about the limitations of our own capabilities.[24] In the documentary about making the song *We Are the World*, one of the best-selling songs of all time, interviews of the performers found almost every singer felt like an imposter, overwhelmed by the other stars in the room. Michael Jackson, Cyndi Lauper, Bruce Springsteen, Paul Simon, Huey Lewis, Ray Charles and Tina Turner were amongst the pops stars who contributed to the song. Even the most accomplished people feel like a fraud at times.

It's also estimated that roughly 85% of people worldwide have suffered low self-esteem at times.[25] Low self-esteem is fed by limiting beliefs that undermine confidence and agency to create positive change for ourselves.

What makes beliefs deeply rooted in our minds is the depth of emotion that is attached to them.

I was told by a friend once to "get out of my own way" when I shared my fears about starting my own business. You may have heard this phrase before. I asked him what he meant, because I couldn't see how I was in my own way.

He explained that when we give in to fears that don't serve us, they get in the way of us doing what we really want. He said, "If we believe the fears are helpful, then they stay in our way". His advice was useful, but it didn't help me find a way to identify and overcome the beliefs that gave rise to the fears that were in my way.

This is what led me to find a practical strategy to search for and remove the limiting beliefs and the fears that kept them rooted deep in my mind and were holding me back from taking on more challenging problems and situations. We can be more in control of how we think and act than we realise. It just takes finding a path to follow.

The Mindset Reset Method is a three-step strategy to identify and replace limiting beliefs with healthier, empowering ones. I was introduced to this idea by Marc Gregory. Its roots are drawn from the principles of cognitive behavioural therapy (CBT), used by psychologists to help treat cognitive distortions. Cognitive distortions are irrational or biased ways of thinking that can lead to negative emotions and problematic behaviours.

Cognitive Behavioural Therapy operates on the basis that thoughts, feelings and behaviours are interconnected, negative thought patterns are often automatic, challenging and reframing negative thoughts provides a pathway to positive change, and gradual and continued exposure to new, healthier thoughts locks in positive change.

Researching the approach further, I learned the key to shifting deeply held beliefs lies in creating new memories and positive emotions that link to a new belief you wish to hold. Simply 'wishing' a new belief to replace an old one or just trying to rationalise it does not produce fast results. Emotions drive our decisions and actions. To create change in our thinking and behaviour, we need to acquire new experiences that create the emotions and memories to draw from as fuel for our new thinking and actions.

It takes far less energy to think and act when you don't have to consciously counteract beliefs that hold you back. Where you have more empowering beliefs than limiting ones when it comes to working on challenging problems, you will find more energy to put towards solving them. This will give you a greater chance of succeeding.

What makes beliefs deeply rooted in our minds is the depth of emotion that is attached to them. For example, if you've never seen fire before and you reach your hand out and touch it, the burn you receive will cause a sharp pain. That pain will lead to a fear of being burned by fire, an intense emotional response.

After this experience, a strong belief would form in your mind that touching fire is very painful, so don't touch it. This new belief helps keep you safe from a new danger you've discovered, by directing your behaviour to avoid touching fire in future.

Thereafter, every time you see fire, your mind, which constantly searches for threats and seeks to protect you, finds that belief and sends signals to your body and nervous system to stay away. It's a subconscious, automatic response driven by a belief and held tight because of the emotion that's associated with it. The stronger the emotion attached to the belief, the stronger your mind and body's reaction to act on it will be.

The exact number of beliefs stored in our minds isn't known. I have read it could be in the hundreds of thousands. Our minds are constantly forming, revising and discarding beliefs based on new information and experiences. We do this both subconsciously and consciously.

There are two ways you can internalise a new belief: from direct experience or from borrowed experience.

1. **Direct experience** is where you personally experience something and internalise a belief about it, such as the fire example above or through direct experience with others.
2. **Borrowed experience** is where you learn from others such as in school, reading books, watching television or listening to what people you trust tell you.

The most deeply held beliefs are where there is a strong fear attached to them. For these beliefs, our mind assigns a high priority to keeping them because of the perceived threat to our safety. Our minds' job is to keep us safe.

Associating a new belief with positive emotions that are equally as strong as the ones attached to a limiting belief you want to replace is the fastest way to remove the hold they have over you.

The Mindset Reset Method

Three steps to replace limiting beliefs and behaviours:

1. **Expose it** – identify and label the limiting beliefs and behaviours that are holding you back.
2. **Switch it** – develop alternative, empowering beliefs and behaviours that better support you and propel you forward.
3. **Bring it in** – bring the new, empowering beliefs into your mindset with new memories, emotions and intentional actions that create and reinforce the change you want to make.

To illustrate how this method works, I share an example that unfolds progressively as the method is explained. I refer to this as Dean's Reset. It's included in a different font to the explanatory text to make it easier to follow. A worksheet showing how the method comes together is included at the end of this chapter.

Step 1: Expose it

The first step in the Mindset Reset Method is to expose the limiting beliefs and behaviours that may be subconsciously sabotaging your attempts to find and solve hard problems to progress your career. Find a quiet space where you can concentrate and reflect. Grab a journal or write what you discover on your computer or phone. Use the Mindset Reset worksheet at the end of this chapter to guide you. The goal is to bring these beliefs to light so you can understand and address them.

Our beliefs are continually shaped by our experiences, both positive and negative. Negative experiences, such as failure or criticism, can lead to the development of limiting beliefs that linger in our subconscious. These beliefs often manifest as self-doubt or self-criticism and can prevent you from reaching your full potential.

To effectively expose limiting beliefs, you need to be completely honest with yourself. We all have imperfections and have areas in need of improvement. We all should wear signs hanging around our necks saying, "Work in Progress!".

Identify triggers

Start by identifying emotional triggers that appear when a challenging problem presents itself—those moments when you experience fear, discomfort, anger, guilt or hesitation. A trigger is just a clue where there is a limiting belief that needs your attention. Just as the pain you feel when you have a splinter lodged in your hand points you to where you need to remove it, a trigger points you to where you need to find the limiting belief that you need to remove.

These triggers reveal underlying limiting beliefs. If you aren't working on a challenging problem right now, think back to other challenging problems you've worked on to search for clues.

For example, you might have noticed you feel anxious when facing challenging tasks or uncomfortable when receiving constructive criticism. You might realise you feel uncomfortable asking for help when you get stuck. Or perhaps you fear making mistakes. All of these triggers are very common.

To track these triggers, keep a journal for a week, noting when and why you experience these emotions.

Consider the following trigger sources to help develop your awareness:
- Being held accountable
- Achieving results
- Collaborating with others
- Receiving criticism
- Experiencing failure
- Feeling a sense of injustice
- Learning something new
- Loss or fear of loss of material things
- Gaining and losing money
- Being respected and having status
- Not having enough or losing time
- Struggling with workload.

DEAN'S RESET

A man, let's call him, Dean, was struggling with his workload. He felt overwhelmed and was working late nights most days, and had been for months. He had a young family and an understanding wife who was able to take the load at home while he worked late, but he constantly felt guilty for not being with them.

It was the first time he really felt he wasn't coping with his workload and didn't know why. He was worried he would start failing and not be able to find opportunities to work on new challenges and problems to grow his experience if he couldn't manage his current responsibilities.

He was discussing this challenge with his mentor, who asked him how he felt about asking for help from others if he was struggling. He grimaced. "I hate asking for help, but I know I should", he said.

His mentor encouraged him to look into the beliefs he had about asking for help to see if they could discover something that was hidden below the surface that he wasn't aware of that caused this reaction.

Identify limiting beliefs

Once you've identified the triggers you want to work on, the next step is to label the limiting beliefs you discover are associated with them. A limiting belief would be, for example, that trusting people always leads to disappointment, so avoid doing it. Limiting beliefs that need to be changed can be expressed as an *action* that leads to a *consequence*.

For example
Action: trusting people.
Consequence: always leads to disappointment.

It's helpful to label the limiting beliefs in the second person, 'you', as though it is being said to you by another person instead of using 'I'. It provides a separation between you as a person and the limiting belief that is not welcome in your mind anymore. If making mistakes makes you feel anxious, your limiting belief could be written as follows: "You believe if you mess up or make a big mistake, you will be fired."

Action: If you mess up or make a big mistake,
Consequence: You will be fired.

Labelling limiting beliefs helps bring them into the open, making it easier to address them.

DEAN'S RESET

Dean spoke to his mentor about his fear of asking for help. His mentor asked him to explain what he believed would happen if he did ask for help. He thought for a minute, then said, "I think it will make me look weak in front of my colleagues and manager and that will hurt my career".

Dean's limiting belief was: "If I ask for help it will make me look weak in front of my colleagues and manager and that will hurt my career".

"Yes", he said. "That's it, I am so worried that if I ask for help people will think I can't cope and I'm not smart enough to do the job."

"And what will that lead to?" his mentor asked. "They will fire me", he said.

Dean had attached an extreme fear of losing his job to asking for help.

After some discussion, Dean wrote the following;

Dean's limiting belief: "If you ask for help, people will think you can't cope and you're not smart enough to do the job and will be fired."

If you're struggling to label a limiting belief, these examples may inspire your thinking:

- I can't handle pressure.
- I'm not good at solving difficult problems.
- I have to solve the problem perfectly or I've failed.
- I don't have time to think things through properly.
- I have to control every aspect of the situation.
- If I don't see immediate progress, I'm on the wrong track.
- I can't trust my instincts, they'll lead me astray.
- If I ask for feedback, it means I don't know what I'm doing.
- I'm too slow at figuring things out.
- I can't afford to take risks, even calculated ones.
- If I don't have the skills or experience to solve a problem effectively, I shouldn't try.
- I'm not creative enough to solve complex problems.
- I have to work alone to get the best results.
- I can't afford to make mistakes, so I should avoid making any decisions until I'm certain.
- If I can't see the entire path forward, I won't be able to solve the problem.
- It's better to avoid the problem than to risk making it worse.
- Complex problems are too overwhelming, I'll never be able to figure them out.
- I need to know every detail before making any move.
- My solutions never work the first time, so it's probably not worth trying.

Identify limiting behaviours

Limiting beliefs left untreated lead to limiting behaviours that reinforce them and create invisible barriers that hold us back. When we are faced with a difficult situation where we need to decide what to do, our mind uses the beliefs most relevant to help make that decision subconsciously. Unless we make the belief and behaviour that we use in these situations conscious, they will continue repeatedly without our awareness.

For the limiting beliefs you have identified, think of all the behaviours that it causes you to make that are not helpful. There may be many.

This work is challenging and can be confronting. If you've lived for any length of time with feelings of anguish about how you will be perceived or judged, as I have, this work is essential to becoming free of the effects of limiting beliefs. Just like a virus, exposing our limiting beliefs to light helps to eliminate them.

> **DEAN'S RESET**
>
> The limiting behaviour Dean chose instead of asking for help was to work long hours alone. This caused him stress and needlessly kept him away from his young family. He desperately wanted to stop making this choice.
> **Dean's limiting behaviour:** "You choose to work long hours to complete your work, causing stress and keeping you from your family, instead of asking for help."

Understand the origins

The most powerful beliefs find their way into our minds through experience or what we have been told by those we trust. Usually, the most deeply rooted ones are from when we were young.

Limiting beliefs left untreated lead to limiting behaviours that reinforce them, which create invisible barriers we can't see that hold us back

Take some time to explore where these limiting beliefs may have originated. Consider past experiences or specific memories that may have contributed to the development of these beliefs. Understanding the origins of limiting beliefs helps you process them and let them go.

When you understand why you have the belief you do, it creates an awareness that helps pave the way for change. When we understand why we act and behave the way we do, particularly where it doesn't serve us, we reduce our resistance to change it.

> ### DEAN'S RESET
>
> Dean recalled an experience he had not long after he entered the workforce. He remembered his first manager in the marketing team where he worked was very critical of him. They were understaffed and had many deadlines to meet, which put his manager under a lot of pressure.
>
> He was writing copy for marketing campaigns and asked his manager for help with a page he was writing for a brochure showcasing the benefits of a new product they were launching.
>
> Dean was new and nervous about how he was performing. He recalled his manager told him he didn't have time to help him that day and he just needed to get the work done and to him by five p.m. that afternoon. And it needed to be done right, he said.
>
> Dean was terrified of him, and worried about losing his job. It took him eight months to find his first job when all his other mates had found one much quicker than that. From that moment on Dean decided not to ask for help if he was struggling, but rather to choose to work harder.

The origins of our limiting beliefs and behaviour can take some time to emerge. Discussing it with a friend or mentor helps, as does spending quiet time alone with no distractions, to allow you mind to find the memories that are most relevant.

Writing down your thoughts, ideas and memories helps shape them into what you need to work on. It's like writing a novel or creating a new product; the final version takes several drafts to get right.

I spend 20 minutes in the morning reflecting on limiting beliefs and behaviours and their origins, to become clear on what mine are. I write them in my journal, and come back to them, refining the language I use until I feel I can't improve on it anymore. You'll know the language is right when you can't think of anything more you can add to express it better.

Step 2: Switch it

Now that you've exposed your limiting beliefs and behaviours, the next step is to create new empowering alternatives to switch them to.

Create new empowering beliefs

For each limiting belief you want to change, write a new, empowering belief that you would prefer over the existing one. If you're using the Mindset Reset Worksheet, create a new sheet for every limiting belief you want to change.

Focus on changing the consequence of the belief. Where you want to do something you haven't done before or are reluctant to do, find a positive consequence that will result from acting on the new belief.

> **When you understand why you have the belief you do, it creates an awareness that helps pave the way for change**

Your new consequence must be realistic and something you can test or have seen is true before. Unrealistic expectations will fail, because when you try to change and it doesn't result in the positive outcome you want, your mind will reject the new belief and revert to the old, limiting one.

It helps to get out of your head and discuss the changes you want to make to your beliefs with a trusted friend or colleague —someone you trust and feel safe to be vulnerable with.

DEAN'S RESET

Dean was initially hesitant to open up and be vulnerable with his peers. Despite his reluctance, he asked two colleagues how they felt about asking for help when they were struggling. They both said they had struggled with asking for help at times.

> His peers told him that since becoming comfortable asking for help, they get a lot more work done and their stress levels had reduced significantly. The validation from his peers was a great boost to his confidence that he was not alone in feeling this way.
>
> After some consideration, Dean wrote the following:
>
> **Dean's old limiting belief:** "You believed if you asked for help, it would make you look weak in front of your colleagues and that would hurt your career."
>
> **Dean's new empowering belief:** "I now believe that asking for help is a sign of strength and can enable me achieve more."

Create new empowering behaviours

Behaviours follow beliefs. Use the same process you've completed with the limiting belief and apply it to all the limiting behaviours you have identified, switching them for empowering ones.

> # DEAN'S RESET
>
> Dean created the following new behaviour he wanted to switch to:
>
> **Old limiting behaviour:** "You chose to work long hours and suffer incredible stress to complete your work instead of asking for help."
>
> **Dean's new empowering behaviour:** "I will now find ways to delegate more and ask for help as I need it."

Step 3: Bring it in

Now it's time to shift gears and bring these new empowering beliefs and behaviours into your mindset and remove the barriers the old, limiting ones put in front of you.

Creating new memories and attaching strong emotions to them neutralises the effects of old, limiting beliefs. Taking consistent action that reinforces these new beliefs locks them into our mindset.

Create new memories and emotions

New memories with positive emotions that support a new belief creates a feedback loop that makes the belief stronger. Over time it means the more you choose to use the new empowering belief and behaviours, the more positive reinforcement you get, making it easier to form new, deeply held habits. Edward de Bono reminds us, "In the end, it is emotion that makes our choices and decisions".

Here are two ways you can create new memories and emotions to draw on to help bring into your mindset a new empowering belief:

1. **Ask people you respect**: supportive words of encouragement from people you trust and respect create powerful new memories and emotions to draw from. For example, ask a manager, mentor, colleague or coach for their thoughts. Explain what you are trying to do and ask what they think of the old belief and the new one you are trying to shift towards. Ask them to provide their experience and tell how it helped them to do what you are trying to do.
2. **Take small, no-risk steps**: find and create experiences that reinforce the benefits and reduce the fear of acting on the new belief. It's important to find no-risk actions. We are most vulnerable to setbacks and self-sabotage when we first start to make a change. If you want to learn to delegate, find a small task to share with a team member with whom you have

a good rapport. If you want to learn how be more comfortable asking for help, try asking for help from someone you trust.

> ## DEAN'S RESET
>
> After asking his peers for their thoughts, Dean asked his new manager, with whom he had a good rapport, what he thought of his limiting belief that asking for help is a sign of weakness. He told Dean, "Asking for help is a sign of leadership and will help me trust you more.
>
> "No one has all the answers. If you are willing to ask for help it means I can trust you more to get your work done and give you larger challenges to work on to grow your career. If I see you not asking for help when you need it, I can't see you progressing very fast."
>
> This experience created a positive set of memories and emotions for Dean to use as fuel to start taking steps to ask for help more and overcome any reluctance from the old beliefs that were holding him back.

New memories and emotions provide motivation to make changes. There are two forms of motivation: 'away-from' and 'moving-towards' motivation.[26] Away-from motivation involves moving away from a pain or discomfort, while moving-towards motivation focuses on achieving positive outcomes.

Away-from motivation is particularly useful to get started. Like running from a burning house, it's an immediate and strong motivation to protect yourself. It helps you act quickly and not delay.

Moving-towards motivation, being future oriented and based on positive outcomes, sustains motivation for a longer period of time. Knowing there will be future positive outcomes, like a carrot being shown in front of a horse, pulls us towards what we want.

To sustain a change to your beliefs, aim to have more of your motivation come from moving-towards goals, memories and emotions. They are more sustainable over a longer period of time. Moving-away motivations are predominantly fear-based and use a lot of energy to maintain.

Write down the new memory and emotions you will use to draw motivation from as you take steps to change your beliefs and behaviours in the Mindset Reset Worksheet.

DEAN'S RESET

The discussion with Dean's manager provided him with both forms of motivation. The fear of not progressing fast if he didn't ask for help was his away-from motivation. The potential to be given larger challenges to work on was his moving-towards motivation. He also felt a strong desire to spend more time with his young family and believed doing that would strengthen his motivation.

Take consistent action

With focus and daily practice, even the most deeply held limiting beliefs can be replaced with empowering ones in a matter of weeks. Develop actions that will keep you focused and doing something each day until you feel the new belief is locked in place and the old one consigned to the dustbin of history. Repetition solidifies new beliefs and creates new behavioural habits.

Research has shown replacing limiting beliefs with new enabling ones can take as little as a few weeks but may also take longer. The time to live the new belief depends on how deeply rooted the original limiting belief is. The question to ask yourself is, "will I be better off with this new enabling belief and rid of the old limiting one?" If the answer is yes, then time doesn't matter as much as committing to making the change you need to happen.

Focus on the practice of letting go of the old belief and encoding the new one with positive behaviours, memories and emotions. Small gains each day create significant change over time. It's the miracle of compounding. Each step forward is one that takes you closer to a mind that is more capable and free.

Consider these actions to assist you.

1. **WRITE IN A JOURNAL**

    Journalling helps you track your progress and reflect on your actions. Spend time each morning outlining your goals for the day and reviewing your previous actions. Consider what you did well, what you could do better and what you learned. This practice helps keep you forward-looking and accountable to yourself.

2. **USE RITUALS**

    Rituals are a powerful way to reinforce new beliefs. Create symbolic acts that represent the release of old beliefs and the acceptance of new ones. For example, you might choose to print your Mindset Rest Worksheet then read it aloud and burn it, symbolising the release of those old beliefs. I've done this many times and it works incredibly well for deeply held limiting beliefs. Obviously, chose to burn the paper in a safe location away from other flammable materials. You can also tear up your worksheet and put it into a bin after reading it.

3. **CREATE A HABIT**

    Michael Phelps, the most decorated swimmer of all time, having won a total of 28 Olympic medals, including 23 golds, three silvers and two bronzes, practiced belief switching.[27] When he was trying to shift negative thoughts and beliefs, he would say the new belief in the form of a positive affirmation every time he walked through a doorway until he felt it had stuck. Do you know how many doorways you walk through every day? When I heard this story, I counted the doorways I walked through for an entire day. I walked through 68, including car doors. Michael understood better than most people the power of repetition to achieve growth and results.

4. **RECRUIT SUPPORT**

   Change is easier when you have someone to both support you and hold you accountable. Find a person you trust that you can share your progress with and ask for feedback and encouragement. And don't give up!

Mindset Reset worksheet – Dean's example

MINDSET RESET WORKSHEET	
1. Expose it	
Trigger: I noticed I feel uncomfortable asking for help when I'm overwhelmed. **Limiting belief:** If you ask for help, people will think you can't cope and are not smart enough to do the job and you will be fired.	**Origin:** My first manager was critical and judgemental when I felt vulnerable. I feared I would lose my job. **Limiting behaviour:** You chose to work long hours, keeping you away from your family to complete your work instead of asking for help.
2. Switch it	
New empowering belief: I now believe asking for help is a sign of strength and can help me achieve more.	**New empowering behaviour:** I will now find ways to delegate more and ask for help as I need it.
3. Bring it in	
New memory: The conversation with my manager and his endorsement that asking for help will build trust with him and lead to new opportunities.	**New emotion:** Positive feeling that changing will be supported and valued by my manager and lead to my career growing. Positive feeling of spending more time with my family.
Actions to lock in new beliefs and behaviours: • No-risk small steps: each week find an opportunity to ask for help when I otherwise wouldn't have. • Repetition: say the new belief to myself when I walk under a doorway. • Ritual: print and rip up this page of old beliefs and daily journalling and reflection to learn from experiences for 21 days. • Discussions with mentor to help reinforce changes.	

CHAPTER 9

Mindset Reset

- Beliefs either hold you back or propel you forward when it comes to solving problems.
- Replacing limiting beliefs and behaviours with empowering ones will unlock your problem-solving potential.
- The Mindset Reset Method provides a simple three-step approach to replace limiting beliefs and behaviours: Expose it, Switch it and Bring it in.
- It can take as little as a day to see improvements and within a few weeks new habits start to be formed.

CHAPTER 10

Sidestep these thinking traps

"We can be blind to the obvious, and we are also blind to our blindness."
Daniel Kahneman

A trap is something that deceives, entangles or confuses you, ultimately restricting your freedom. Something we need to be on the lookout for and avoid. The most pernicious traps in problem-solving are the invisible cognitive biases, 'thinking traps', that can distort how you perceive situations, weigh evidence and make decisions. These traps are hard to spot in ourselves if we aren't aware they exist. They create blindness even when we believe we can see perfectly clearly.

Cognitive biases are shortcuts the brain takes to save energy, but they can cloud your judgement and lead you down unproductive paths if you're unaware of them. For example, relying too heavily on first impressions, overvaluing recent events, or fearing loss more than valuing potential gain can steer you away from effective solutions and reduce your adaptability.

> **The most pernicious traps in problem-solving are the invisible cognitive biases, 'thinking traps', that can distort how you perceive situations, weigh evidence and make decisions.**

By understanding these biases, you gain more control over how you approach and dissect problems. Recognising a bias allows you to manage its influence. Becoming aware of the mental shortcuts you're likely to take and their downsides helps you to better question assumptions and adopt a more nuanced approach to problem-solving. For example, knowing that confirmation bias may lead you to favour information that supports your initial opinion encourages you to seek out diverse viewpoints or data that challenge your perspective.

These are the most common thinking traps I've come across when problem-solving, how to recognise them and what you can do to counteract them.

Anchoring bias

Relying too heavily on the first piece of information received (the 'anchor') when making decisions.

Psychologists Daniel Kahneman and Amos Tversky introduced anchoring bias in 1974, observing that people often rely too heavily on the first piece of information they come across (the 'anchor'), which affects how they think, feel and make judgements. In negotiation, the first offer is used as the anchor point by savvy strategists to try and influence the outcome of the negotiation in their favour.

Indicators

Evidence of anchoring bias includes over-reliance on initial data or sticking to first estimates despite new information emerging that suggests adjustments are essential and justified, with no other mitigation available.

Countermeasures

Train yourself and coach teams you work with to view initial data as only one of many potential reference points and establish processes for regular reassessment as new information arises.

Attribution bias

Misjudging causes of behaviour by attributing it to personality traits rather than external factors.

Attribution bias refers to the tendency to misinterpret the causes of behaviours and events, leading to skewed perceptions and poor decisions. This bias shows up when people attribute success to predominantly internal factors, such as their personal skill or intelligence, while also blaming failures on external factors, such as bad luck or situational constraints.

Indicators

Signs of attribution bias include where people tend to regularly attribute team failures to individual shortcomings rather than consider other contextual factors; excessive criticism of colleagues based on perceived character flaws; and a lack of recognition for the role of situational influences on outcomes.

Countermeasures

To mitigate attribution bias, practice empathy, seek to understand the context behind behaviours, and focus on constructive feedback that considers skills as well as managing external factors and communicating in advance when expectations will not be met.

Availability bias

Overestimating the importance of information that is most readily available in memory, rather than what's most relevant.

The availability bias or heuristic is where you overestimate the importance or likelihood of events based on how easily examples come to mind. This bias can lead to skewed perceptions of reality, as we tend to judge the frequency or probability of an event based on recent exposure or vivid experiences rather than on broader statistical evidence. It forces your mind to think about that one event and overweight its importance on the future. While often useful for quick decision-making, it can result in flawed judgements and poor decision-making in various contexts, especially when assessing risks or making predictions about how urgent a problem is or how suitable a solution may be to solve it.

Indicators

A reliance on anecdotal evidence, overemphasis on recent events, and impulsive decision-making based on recent experiences are common indicators.

Countermeasures

Encourage data-driven analysis that goes beyond recent trends. Be mindful of jumping to conclusions based on limited but emotionally powerful information. Develop a structured framework for data collection to ensure that decisions are based on balanced and well-founded understanding.

Bandwagon effect

Adopting beliefs or behaviours because others are doing so, often at the expense of independent thought.

The bandwagon effect occurs when people adopt certain behaviours, beliefs or opinions primarily because they perceive that others are doing the same. It's common to defer to experience and seniority, and even considered polite and good manners in some cultures. However, this can significantly compromise problem-solving, particularly where it leads to avoiding the real problem or choosing solutions that are preferred by one party and not the most valuable based on merit. This bias can lead to conformity and a lack of critical analysis in problem-solving and decision-making processes.

This tendency is particularly pronounced in environments where social validation is highly sought-after, leading people to prioritise group consensus over independent thought. I was warned to be wary of the HIPPO's opinion by senior partners I used to work for. That's the highest paid person's opinion. If people deferred without question to this person's opinion, I was to be aware there were likely other options that needed to be considered.

Indicators

Indicators of the bandwagon effect include following trends without personal evaluation, excessive reliance on popular opinion when making choices, and a reluctance to voice dissenting views in group settings.

Countermeasures

To combat the bandwagon effect, cultivate a culture of independent thinking, seek diverse viewpoints, and encourage open discussions that value critical analysis over consensus.

Certainty effect

Overvaluing outcomes that are perceived as certain while undervaluing those that are probable, even when the probable options offer greater overall value.

We tend to give disproportionate weight to outcomes that are guaranteed compared to those that are uncertain, even when the uncertain outcomes may offer a higher expected value. This ingrained bias towards certainty can prevent you from pursuing slightly riskier but potentially more rewarding opportunities, leading to safer but less innovative options even when there are better alternatives.

Imagine you have two marketing strategies to solve the problem of achieving growth targets for your business:

Option A: a virtually certain revenue gain of $500,000.

Option B: a 50% chance of earning $1.2 million or a 50% chance of earning $200,000.

Even though Option B has the potential to provide a higher return, the certainty effect often leads people to prefer the guaranteed, smaller gain of Option A. This is because the certainty of receiving $500,000 feels safer and more reassuring than the risk of getting nothing with Option B, despite the higher average expected return.

Indicators

Signs of the certainty effect include excessive risk aversion, a preference for guaranteed outcomes, and reluctance to explore options with uncertain but potentially beneficial results.

Countermeasures

To counteract the certainty effect, actively seek information on probabilities and outcomes, focus on long-term benefits rather than short-term certainties, and use decision-making frameworks, such as multi-criteria decision analysis, that evaluate options objectively.

Confirmation bias

Focusing on information that confirms pre-existing beliefs, leading to selective reasoning.

Confirmation bias is the tendency to search for, interpret and recall information in a way that confirms your pre-existing beliefs. People often overlook evidence that contradicts their initial ideas, which limits their ability to consider alternative viewpoints. Confirmation bias unconsciously narrows your focus, because it forces you to selectively gather data that supports your assumptions rather than questioning or expanding them. It's tempting because it avoids the potential of additional work that would result from contrary viewpoints or the shame of being 'wrong'.

Indicators

Look out when you notice yourself or others seeking information that aligns with a favoured solution, ignoring contradictory data, or dismissing dissenting opinions without fair and objective consideration.

Countermeasures

Encourage diverse viewpoints and implement a 'devil's advocate' approach to challenge assumptions. In group settings, assigning roles to critically evaluate proposed ideas can help mitigate confirmation bias.

Framing effect

Making decisions based on how information is presented, rather than on the information itself.

The framing effect describes the tendency for people to make different decisions based on how information is presented, or 'framed', even when the underlying facts are the same. If a problem is framed as potentially incurring a loss, research has found you're more likely to take bigger risks to solve it. But if it's framed as achieving a gain, you'll probably play it safe and take less risk. This means the same problem can lead to completely different approaches and potential outcomes simply based on how it's presented.

Imagine the company you're working for is considering a new marketing strategy. You're presented with two options for launching a promotional campaign, each framed differently:

1. **Loss frame:** if we don't implement this new marketing strategy, we could lose $500,000 in additional revenue.
2. **Gain frame:** by implementing this new marketing strategy, we could gain $500,000 in additional revenue.

Even though the potential outcome is the same—a $500,000 gain—the way the information is framed will invoke different emotions and potential actions.

In the loss frame, the focus is on what could be lost if the strategy isn't adopted. This tends to trigger a stronger emotional response due to the fear of loss. People presented with this type of framing feel pressured to take more aggressive actions, such as quickly adopting the strategy or investing additional resources to avoid the loss. Fear drives impulsive problem-solving decisions.

In the gain frame, the emphasis is on achieving more. This framing tends to lead to people to be more cautious, evaluating the strategy more carefully to ensure it's worth the investment, because the focus is on achieving some additional benefit rather than avoiding losing what they have.

Indicators
Become aware of how problems, evidence, options and solutions are presented to you. If the way information is presented emphasises the downside as the problem, it's more likely to inspire a stronger emotional reaction and urgency, which can lead to poor decisions.

Countermeasures
To counteract the framing effect, practice restating the information presented using the opposite perspective. Instead of avoiding a loss, restate it as achieving a gain and consider if that would change your perspective on the situation and the actions you would take.

Loss aversion

Focusing more on avoiding losses than on gaining equivalent benefits, which can lead to overly cautious decisions.

Loss aversion describes the preference of people to avoid losses rather than acquire equivalent gains. Most people hate losing more than they enjoy winning. Research shows that losses are felt more intensely than gains of the same magnitude. For example, losing $10,000 feels more painful than the pleasure derived from gaining $10,000. The extent of attachment we have to what may be lost amplifies the loss aversion bias. This thinking trap can make us overly cautious when facing problems, sometimes even freezing us in place and missing opportunities for ourselves and the organisations we work for.

Indicators

Signs of loss aversion include an unwillingness to take risks, holding on to unviable strategies longer than necessary, or focusing excessively on potential losses during discussions about problems and the strategies to solve them.

Countermeasures

To mitigate against loss aversion, practice reframing potential losses as learning opportunities, focus on long-term benefits of risk-taking, and develop a more balanced view of gains and losses.

Overconfidence bias

Being overly confident of one's own abilities, leading to underestimating risks or challenges.

Overconfidence bias was first observed and researched by Baruch Fischhoff in the 1970s. He found that people frequently overestimate their knowledge and abilities because we tend to over trust fragile assumptions, narrow our estimates of future outcomes, and mistake our expertise for immunity to error. This bias can lead to overlooking potential risks, disregarding feedback, or making uninformed decisions, as people assume their skills or knowledge are sufficient without verifying them.

Indicators

Indicators include frequent dismissal of others' insights, resistance to double-checking facts, and underestimating complexity in approaching and solving problems and in decision-making.

Countermeasures

Use measures that seek out objective data or contrary views. Checklists, alternative scenarios and simulations are useful to verify if confidence is well founded.

Sunk cost fallacy

Continuing a course of action because of past investments (time, money or resources) rather than considering future benefits.

The sunk cost fallacy is the tendency to continue doing or having something once an investment in money, time or resources has been made, despite new evidence suggesting that the cost of continuing outweighs the benefits. It's a manifestation of loss aversion, where the emotional weight of past investments inhibits rational decision-making about future actions. We prefer not to experience feeling loss and construct blind spots to consider giving up what we have previously invested in.

Indicators

Signs of the sunk cost fallacy may include justifying further investment in failing projects due to prior expenditures, reluctance to abandon outdated strategies, and a focus on past costs rather than future potential.

Countermeasures

Establish clear criteria for success and objectively and regularly measure against it. Encourage an open and positive challenge culture where outside observations are welcomed and debated. Set a stop loss policy for investment, consider opportunity cost as well as actual cost in considering options. Use reframing to consider the alternative; for example, instead of saying, "we have invested so much already, we can't stop" say "we have invested a lot and will leverage the learning and capabilities from that investment in these other ways".

Status quo bias

Favouring current conditions and resisting change due to fear of the unknown.

Status quo bias is the preference for keeping things the same or maintaining current conditions rather than making changes, even when potential improvements are available and desirable. It's the most common and challenging barrier in solving challenging problems that require introducing anything new. We naturally fear change initially, until we can see and are convinced the change will benefit us more than what we have or what we do. It's a survival mechanism that's deeply ingrained in our mindset.

Indicators

Signs of status quo bias includes resisting or avoiding discussions about change; reluctance to consider new technologies or ideas not currently embraced; or downplaying evidence from outside the organisation that suggests there are better alternatives to what is being done currently. Be on the lookout for language that suggests fear may be lurking behind how people respond to problems and potential solutions that infer changes to what they know or do.

Countermeasures

Develop your empathy radar to problems and potential solutions that may involve changing how people think, behave and affect what they have. Becoming aware of how people may interpret new information as a threat will lead you to frame it in a way that acknowledges this fear and seeks to address it with compassion and humility —traits that help built trust when people feel threatened.

CHAPTER 10:

Sidestep these thinking traps

- We are all susceptible to cognitive biases or 'thinking traps' when solving challenging problems. These traps can undermine our ability to think and act clearly, causing us to make poor decisions.
- Awareness of common thinking traps and recognising their warning signs is the most effective way to counteract them.
- The most common thinking traps I've seen are anchoring bias, attribution bias, bandwagon effect, certainty effect, confirmation bias, framing effect, loss aversion, overconfidence bias, sunk cost fallacy and status quo bias.

CHAPTER 11

Prevent 'Dark Marks'

"An ounce of prevention is worth a pound of cure."
John F. Kennedy

Mark was an ambitious young camera operator starting out his movie making career in Hollywood by honing his skills shooting music videos. He was in his early thirties and ambitious, eager to forge a path into the feature film world.

The job of a camera operator is to capture images the way the director wants them. There's a lot of uncertainty and long hours working in the film industry, as well as a load of technical challenges and pressure to get it right. But it was a job he loved, and he was keen to make his mark.

Filming costs a lot of money. The cost of hiring actors and crew, constructing sets, renting locations, transporting and feeding the cast and crew, making costumes and arranging for insurances etc. can be astronomically high. People in the industry work hard to make sure there are minimal extra takes to save time and money. For a high-budget Hollywood blockbuster, the cost for one hour of filming can be upwards of $250,000.

It was a bright sunny Tuesday in Oregon and filming was due to start at 11 am. It was the first day of a week-long shoot. Mark arrived at eight a.m. and collected his gear from the camera truck. He studied the storyboards and went over the anticipated shot list for the day. He was filled with adrenaline; it was big film gig for him and he was pinching himself for finally starting to live his dream.

For this filming sequence they were using analogue film to shoot the scenes, rather than digital. It was a choice the director had made to make the film appear more 'indie'. Mark needed to use a new can of film for every scene and record the take number, time and date to match the script to make the job of editing the film easier later on.

As they were filming outside, Mark had to fit 'French flags' (sunshades) to the camera lens to stop the sunlight from overexposing the film. It was a job he had done hundreds of times before. He chose a four-sided sunshade to use with an adjustable flap on the left- and right-hand side of the lens as well as the top and bottom. Each of the four flaps could be adjusted independently to protect and shield the lens from sun glare.

Filming continued right up until 10 p.m. that evening. After the final scene had ended, Mark packed the cans of film he had used during the day and placed them in the nearby camera truck, which delivered them to the lab the next day for processing.

Two days later, the film had been developed and was returned to the editing team to look over. It was another filming day at around 10 a.m. when the director, looking red faced and flustered, rushed over to Mark who was setting up for the day's filming, yelled, "Mark, this is f*cked. We have to reschedule and reshoot an entire day of filming".

"What?" Mark said.

"Every frame from the first day's filming has a dark strip at the top of it", the director exclaimed, his hands shooting above his head in despair.

Mark was dumbfounded. How could this have happened? He ran through all the possibilities in his mind, his heart now racing so fast he could feel it in his throat.

Then it suddenly dawned on him. The top sunshade flap must have dropped about 10 mm below where he had set it, causing the top of each frame of film to be black as it was exposed to the back of the sunshade. He mustn't have tightened the screw that kept the sunshade in place enough when he set up the camera for the day.

While filming was underway, he was focusing on shooting the scene correctly. He didn't think to check if the sunshades were correctly set. There was no solution to this problem other than reshooting every scene. It was critical to the movie plot and couldn't be scripted out. The extra cost would be substantial.

The next day the affected scenes were refilmed without a hitch. Mark paid careful attention to the positioning of the sunshades this time and thought through every small detail that could possibly cause the film to not be properly exposed. He made a checklist so he wouldn't forget anything. It was a painful but valuable lesson.

Searching for and preventing significant future problems that you are responsible for is smart.

At the next location two weeks later, the film's producer asked the entire crew to assemble prior to filming getting underway. He ran through how the production was tracking and what was scheduled.

He said, "You are all well aware of the setback we had two weeks ago. I want each and every one of you to double- and triple-check what could go wrong and fix it before we start filming. I don't want any more 'Dark Marks' on this film."

The crew roared with nervous laughter, while Mark winced. The producer added, "We are only as good as the problems we can foresee. Where you know of a problem we can't fix if it happens, do whatever it takes to make sure it doesn't happen."

Mark had great difficulty losing his new nickname, 'Dark Mark'. For years after, Mark retold his 'Dark Mark' story to the production crew of films he worked on as a reminder to avoid preventable problems arising. Mark went on to make many more movies. He didn't let this setback take him off course from pursuing his dream of working on major Hollywood movies.

The principle from this story is to search for potential unsolvable problems beforehand and take steps to prevent them.

Questions to help you find and prevent and unsolvable problems:

- What are the types of consequences my work or responsibilities could have for others, my business, other businesses, my employers and my reputation?
- How big could these consequences be if they happened once, twice, or regularly? Consider a range of impacts such as financial cost, human injury and business interruption, for example.
- How could each of these consequences arise? What would have to happen or not happen for them to occur?
- Of the causes of the significant consequences that could occur, which are in my control and which are not?
- For causes within my control, how can I make sure they don't happen? Can I use checklists, training, simulations, physical controls such as barriers or safety equipment, protocols such as announcing an event will happen so everyone is aware of it?
- For causes not in my control, how can I make sure others who can control it prevent it from occurring or, if no one can, then how can I transfer the consequences to someone else, such as an insurer?
- Is there anyone with more experience and expertise who can help me understand what future problems and their consequences could be? Would I feel better prepared if I asked for help?

CHAPTER 11

Prevent 'Dark Marks'

- Proactively find potential problems and prevent them when the consequences would be intolerable.
- Use tools like checklists and protocols to prevent unsolvable problems.
- Turn screw-ups (we all make them) into learning stories to improve the problem-solving capabilities of your team and organisation.

A Problem Hunter's Strategy

OVERVIEW

A problem-solving strategy is simply a method to help move you from where you are to where you want to be. It helps to organise effort efficiently, allocate resources and guide decision-making. Having a strategy makes the job of solving problems easier and saves time. Why can't we just wing it and make it up as we go, you might be thinking? Well, you can. I have, many times. But what I have learned is winging it is the least efficient, least reliable and most stressful way to solve problems.

In this section I'll introduce you to the 3R Problem Solving Strategy. It's been developed to apply to any workplace problem you need to solve. It combines my 25 years of problem-solving experience with the best of what I've learned from top-tier management consulting firms, marketing experts, entrepreneurs, medical professionals, engineers and artists.

A case study flows through the first three chapters of this section to bring the 3R Problem Solving Strategy to life. It follows Alison, a Human Resources Manager, who has sought out and accepted the challenge of solving a problem for her CEO that is a long way outside her comfort zone. I refer to this case study in the following chapters as Alison's Problem.

Solving challenging problems will test even the most stoic person. We all need help at times. How to be more open to asking for and receiving help is a skill that I'll show you how to master. Finally, a young beer baron will show you the value of one of the most versatile and widely practiced problem-solving techniques—inversion. This is where you purposely look at problems from the opposite perspective to identify radical and innovative solutions

3R Problem Solving Strategy

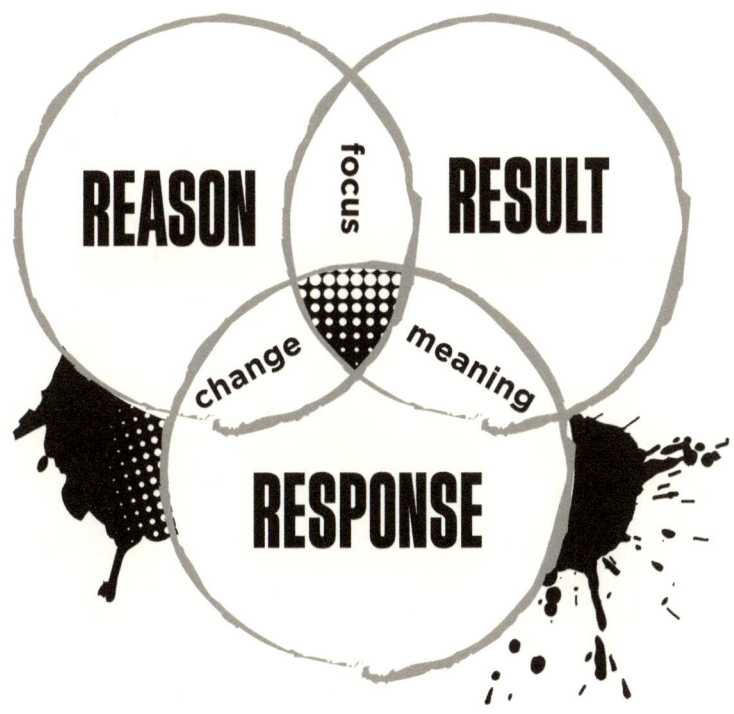

Three steps to help you solve any problem:

1. Understand the **Reason** you have a problem.
2. Choose the **Result** you need to achieve.
3. Develop the **Response** that best delivers the result you need.

Benefits of using the 3R Problem Solving Strategy:
- Gives you **focus** to solve the right problem.
- Creates **meaning** and motivation to solve the problem.
- Delivers **change** that targets the root causes of the problem to deliver the result you need.

CHAPTER 12

Understand the Reason

"Being able to accurately identify what the problem is and allocate resources accordingly is the single skill that has made me the highest return in my life."
Alex Hormozi

Problems have many names. Marketing professionals call them 'pain points'. Software engineers refer to them as 'bugs'. Product development professionals refer to them as 'defects'. Management professionals refer to them as 'issues' or 'challenges'. Aeronautical engineers refer to them as 'malfunctions', 'anomalies' or 'faults'. Human Resources professionals refer to them as 'concerns'. Finance professionals refer to them as 'discrepancies' or 'variances'. Manufacturing managers refer to them as 'bottlenecks'.

No matter what flavour of problem you may have, they all share similar characteristics. There is a challenging situation, an important result to achieve and a solution that needs to be found. In this chapter we focus on the first part of a solving a problem—understanding the difficult situation you find yourself or your business in. This is what I refer to as understanding the *reason* you have a problem.

All too often I've seen well-meaning teams rush to develop solutions to an ill-defined problem that wastes time and resources and frustrates everyone involved. As Albert Einstein said, "If I had only one hour to save the world, I would spend fifty-five minutes defining the problem, and only five minutes finding the solution". The problem you define is the problem you solve.

Research has shown that poorly defined problems in organisations leads to significant waste of resources, inefficiencies and lost time.

> **The problem you define is the problem you solve.**

A study by McKinsey found that unclear problem definitions cause substantial delays to solving problems and can create 'solution tunnels', where teams fixate on specific approaches rather than understanding the root problem.[28] In engineering fields 'defining the problem' significantly impacts a solution's success rate. It prevents 'problem blindness', where teams skip defining the issue and dive straight into solutions. Spending time clearly defining the problem up front means you will more likely avoid these pitfalls, and not waste time and resources.

To understand the reason for a problem and define it well, you need to look past symptoms and search for the real causes and whether they matter.

To begin to understand and define a problem, you need to:

1. Describe the situation.
2. Determine whether it matters.
3. Find the causes.

Completing these actions will paint the first part of the picture of what the real problem is and give you the reason to take further action. The second part of a problem is choosing the result you need. Combining them gives you clarity on the problem you need to solve.

This first step will help you determine whether you have a pool of water on the floor from someone's water bottle spilling that just needs to be mopped up, or if you have a slow-leaking roof that requires a tradesman to repair it. Both situations produce the same symptom—a pool of water on the floor. But the actions you need to take to solve them will differ dramatically.

This chapter will guide you through the process of uncovering the 'why' behind your problem, helping you define it well and setting the stage to choose the right result and the best response to achieve it.

Describe the situation

Problems create tension; a frustration; a gap between what we experience now and what we would prefer in the future. Something needs to change. Understanding a problem starts with describing the situation you find yourself in.

There are four types of problems:

1. **Pioneering problems:** where you want to do something but aren't.
2. **Acquisition problems:** where you want to have something but don't.
3. **Disruption problems:** where you don't want to do something but are.
4. **Burden problems:** where you don't want to have something but do.

Consider the situation you have and decide how best to describe it using one of the four problem types.

Pioneering problems

Where you want to do something but aren't

This is an inaction problem. You are not doing something important that you want to be doing. In emerging organisations with few established systems and methods there is an abundance of pioneering problems that need solving to create the foundational methods for working, to adapt and grow the business rapidly.

For more mature organisations, where ways of working have been largely established, pioneering problems come in the form of adapting to changing external forces such as requirements from new laws and regulations, business model shifts, repairing processes that break, and a drive for productivity and innovation.

The core of this type of problem is the need to introduce new actions and behaviours and develop new skills and capabilities.

Examples:
- We want to invoice new customers within two hours for work performed, but don't have the capability to do it.
- We want to implement a same-day delivery service for rural areas, but are capacity constrained.
- We want to launch a personalised onboarding experience for new clients within 48 hours of contract signing to create a unique first impression and differentiate us from competitors, but currently aren't able to.
- We want to scale our business quickly and maintain a five-star customer service experience, but don't know how.

Acquisition problems

Where you want to have something but don't

This is where you define your problem as needing something you currently lack or requiring improvements to what already exists. This might involve securing additional resources such as funding, new locations, intellectual property, partners, products, talent or technology.

These types of problems result from a deficiency in what you have when compared to what you need. This is either because something that existed is no longer available, such as a fire or flood restricting access to sites and buildings and needing to be replaced, or where aspirations for a better future create a gap from what exists today, such as a larger office space to accommodate a growing business.

The core of this type of problem is obtaining something new or more of what already exists.

Examples:
- We want $50 million more sales to achieve budget, but don't have a sufficient pipeline of leads.
- We want more products shipped per day to meet our delivery targets, but can't increase our picking speeds.
- We want better-clarity screens for our new product to improve viewing ease, but don't know the right specifications or suppliers to achieve this.
- We want to be confident we won't experience future data loss, but are reaching the limits of our storage capacity, which is concerning.

Disruption problems

You don't want to do something but are

These problems arise when you are doing something that is suboptimal; where what you do is creating errors, additional costs, poor quality or bottlenecks. An established way you are working needs to change.

The core of this type of problem is unlearning what has been done and introducing new actions and behaviours and developing new skills and capabilities. It's a more challenging problem than pioneering, because changing embedded behaviours and replacing them with new ones requires both letting go of the past and learning something new. We fear losing what we have and know how to do more than just struggling to learn what we don't know.

Examples:
- We manually process invoices, which is inefficient and is costing us too much.
- We keep running out of stock each month and are losing sales.
- Our average response time to complaints is over five days and this is frustrating customers.
- We are currently being paid by our customers 30 days after our invoice date, which is too slow.

Burden problems

You don't want to have something but do

These problems arise when the assets, resources and commitments you have no longer perform as expected or are surplus to what is now required. What is needed is beyond what is currently available.

The core of this type of problem is holding on to something unwanted, which hinders your ability to move forward, innovate or improve your situation. It feels like you're carrying a dead weight that needs to be liberated.

Examples:
- We have 3,000 square metres of excess warehouse space which is costing us too much to hold.
- We have a customer satisfaction rating of 2.5, which has slipped from 4.9 and is impacting sales.
- We have old and unreliable equipment which is breaking down too often and slowing down our productivity.
- We have debt that is more expensive than what is currently available in the market and it is impacting our bottom line.

What you first describe as the problem will change and evolve as you better understand it and the causes that contribute to it. Write down a description of the problem you have using the most appropriate language to describe it. Iterate that as you learn more and validate it with stakeholders and key decision makers.

Frame your problem at the right level

The level at which you position your problem matters. It sets the context for how you will investigate and try and solve it. What we focus on directs our energy and attention. This first step requires you to zoom in to describe the problem, but also zoom out to make sure you describe it at the right level so an appropriate range of options can be considered later.

Have you ever parked on the side of a road that had metered parking? Most of us have. Modern parking meters have software that allows payments to be taken by credit cards. It's a key requirement of the parking meter to do its job.

My friend Pete Seligman, a Sydney-based entrepreneur and investor shared this problem-framing story with me. At the time, he was helping coach the leadership team of one of his investments that manufactured and supplied parking meters to local councils. The software that supported credit card payments had stopped working. The business had written its own software program for the parking meters to allow it to connect with third party banking systems to process credit card payments.

He told me his leadership team had initially defined their situation as the following:

"We want the *software we developed* for our parking meters to support credit card transactions."

Hearing this initial framing of the situation, Pete asked the leadership team, "Why are we just focusing on wanting *our software* to work?"

This question helped the leadership team reframe the problem at a much higher level. They revised their definition of the problem to be:

"*Our parking meters* aren't able to collect payment via credit card transactions because they cannot connect to banking systems."

The initial description focused on wanting the *software they wrote* to process credit card transactions to collect payments, implying they wanted to just fix their software. The reframed description focused more broadly as *wanting their parking meters* to process credit card transactions to collect payment.

By using the first description of the situation, the problem-solving process would have focused exclusively on how to fix the in-house software. Choosing this path would have closed off other, potentially more valuable solution options to consider, such as replacing the in-house developed software with an alternative provided by a specialist third party.

It was an unconscious sunk cost bias that prevented the team from considering replacing their software as part of the solution. A sunk cost bias is where people continue investing time, money, or resources into a decision or project based on the amount they have already invested, rather than on its current or future value. We have a tendency to want to avoid losses, so we continue to invest rather than cut our loses if there is a better option.

Take your time to consider how to 'frame' your current situation and whether it is at the right level to give you the best range of options you need to solve it. Don't rush this thinking step. Consider any hidden biases that may be influencing the way in which the situation is being defined. Run through multiple iterations of the description until you are comfortable it has been defined clearly and at the most appropriate level.

ALISON'S PROBLEM

Alison is a Human Resources Manager and works in a fashion wholesaling business that sells clothing to retail boutiques and chains across Australia and Singapore. It's a growing business with over 150 people. Alison has worked in her current role for a little over two years, is confident in what she is doing, but feels ready to pursue further growth.

Alison discussed her desire to be given a new challenge with her boss, Mike, at her last performance review. He said he would help find an opportunity for her to work on, and has now found one. It will see Alison work directly with the CEO, Jessie.

Understanding the situation

Alison met with Jessie on a Monday morning. She had met Jessie a few times before, but this was her first one-on-one meeting with her. She was both excited and incredibly nervous. Jessie explained to Alison, "I would like your help to get our customers to pay earlier than they do. They currently pay us 30 days after our invoice date. I need it to be much sooner. We need to get cash in the door faster within the next few months." she said. She added, "We have long-term contracts with our customers which makes it challenging to find a fast solution".

Alison had not worked on a problem like this before. It sounded simple enough, but well outside her comfort zone of dealing with human resources matters. It was exactly what she was looking for. Alison asked Jessie, "Who can I work with to better understand the problem?" Jessie replied, "Talk to Jim, our Financial Controller, who will have more information for you. Come back and brief me on what you believe the problem is we need to solve after you've spoken to Jim", she said before getting up to leave. "No problem", replied Alison.

Alison's initial description of the problem

Our customers pay us 30 days after our invoice date which is too slow. We need it to be much sooner.

Determine whether it matters

A problem isn't a problem that matters unless the consequences of inaction are more than the effort and cost of taking action to solve it. A problem needs to matter for it to make sense to solve it. It gives context to the solutions that need to be developed and the constraints that will be placed on finding and delivering them. It provides a clear focus on what's at stake to direct efforts to find the right solution.

There are four core problem consequences to consider whether a problem matters and needs to be addressed: value, time, status and wellbeing.

Value

What is the financial impact? Is this a one-off or will the situation persist, and for how long? Does it reduce sales, increase costs, reduce asset values or increase liabilities? Does it affect the cash flow of the business?

Quantifying the financial impact of the problem provides a powerful and easily understandable reason a problem matters.

Status

How does the problem affect intangible but important areas such as values, principles, reputation, compliance with laws or critical business conditions like regulatory approvals, licences, customer ratings and credit ratings?

How does it affect future awards, such as employer of choice or customer service rankings?

Damage to reputation, loss of licences or failure to meet contract conditions can significantly affect future performance and a business' survival.

Time

Does the problem lead to additional time being spent or reduce the time available to accomplish goals and priorities? If time is a critical resource, a problem that consumes valuable time can have a significant impact. When might the problem materialise? Is it a near term-impact or somewhere off into the distance?

Wellbeing

How could the problem affect physical safety or mental wellbeing? What impact could it have on the natural environment or wildlife?

People and the environment we live in are critical resources to protect.

By considering how a problem affects value, status, time and wellbeing, you can determine whether it's worth investing further time to understand its causes and find a solution.

Where the impacts can't be determined conclusively, use your best estimate. The assumptions you use and how you've arrived at your estimate will help provide confidence your assessment is believable.

Where a problem doesn't create an impact that matters, you can argue that it isn't a problem worth solving.

ALISON'S PROBLEM

Alison arranged to meet with Jim, the Financial Controller. Alison asked Jim, "Why is it important that we get paid by our customers earlier than 30 days?" Jim replied, "For the next two years, cash flow is tight and being paid 30 days after invoice date could mean will mean we run out of cash at points within that period, or come very close".

This sounded very significant, Alison thought. "How much faster do we need to be paid?" she asked. "Within 15 days of invoice date tops", Jim replied. "That's clear, thank you", Alison said. "How long do I have before we need to have payments being received within 15 days?" she asked. "We really need to be seeing this improvement by September, within 90 days", Jim said. "What if we can't deliver within 90 days?" Alison asked.

Jim lowered his voice and said, "If we consistently fall short of our cash flow targets by 15%, we will be in trouble with our banks. That could mean the funding they provide us to pay for stock in advance of sales may be withdrawn." This is a problem that really matters, Alison thought to herself.

"Who can I talk to, to understand why we aren't being paid at 15 days now?" Alison asked Jim. "Go and talk to Sandra in Sales, as she knows about how our customer contracts work", he said.

Does the problem matter?
Alison now understood how serious the problem was and how urgent it was to find and implement a solution. With this knowledge in mind, she was ready to take the next step to understand the causes of the current situation.

Revised problem statement
Alison incorporated her understanding of why the problem mattered into a revised problem statement.

"We are currently being paid 30 days after invoice date, which is too slow. We need to be paid in 15 days or less starting in September, which is 90 days from now. This is a significant problem that affects our cash flow and the future of the business."

Find the causes

When you are confident you understand the current situation and why it matters, your next action is to understand its causes. The causes of a problem provide the targets to develop solutions. They reveal exactly where you need to focus your effort. If you don't know what's really driving the situation, you'll end up tackling symptoms instead of solving the actual problem. Imagine trying to fix a sinking boat by just bailing out the water. Without finding the leak and plugging it, you're just buying yourself a little more time before the boat goes down. When you identify the cause, you know exactly where to aim. It lets you focus your resources, energy and time on what will make the biggest impact.

Causes of problems are often hidden behind what's most visible. Symptoms like missed deadlines, low sales, or poor customer reviews are easy to see. But if you only deal with what's on the surface, the deeper issues will continue to lurk below. For example, you might see customer complaints about slow response times, but the real cause could be a lack of training or unclear processes within the support team.

You want to go beyond what's obvious, find out why things are really happening, and uncover the patterns or structures driving the issue.

A significant challenge for electric vehicle take-up is battery charging time. It can take more than 30 minutes to recharge a battery fully. This contributes greatly to the 'range anxiety' people have about these vehicles. The long time it takes to charge an EVs battery and the limited number of charging stations available means when you need to charge your vehicle, you may have to wait for a considerable time to do so. People find this very annoying.

One of the reasons for the long charge times is the heat that builds up in the battery when fast charging. As EV batteries start to charge rapidly, they get hot. When this happens the battery management electronics in the car calls for the charge power to be throttled back, because heat damages the battery.

Finding a way to prevent the battery heating up while fast charging provided the target to help develop solutions to this problem. Niche EV battery maker Nyobolt used their understanding of the cause of lithium-ion batteries heating up during fast charging to find such a solution. By changing the formulation of the anode (the negative electrode of the battery that plays a critical role in the charge and discharge processes in each battery cell), their batteries could be fast-charged without heating up. This change meant they could charge their batteries from 10% to 80 % in less than five minutes instead of the typical 30 minutes. This created a potential game-changing solution for this industry. Understanding the real causes of a problem gives you the fuel to find solutions that work.

Knowing why a problem exists helps you figure out why it's worth fixing. When you understand the root causes, it's easier to connect the dots for others and build a case for action. It's not just about saying, "We have a problem". It's about saying, "Here's what's causing it, and why we need to solve it now".

This level of clarity gives people confidence in dedicating time and resources to solving problems. It shows that you're not just reacting, but making informed decisions based on a solid understanding of what's actually going on. People rally behind a cause when they know the reasoning behind it and can see how taking action to address the cause will make a real difference. Finding the causes of problems creates meaning. It's why people donate to disease research. It creates meaning when we find out why problems exist. Because when we do, it opens the door for solutions to be found.

Two techniques that can help you pinpoint the causes of problems are the 5-Whys method and hypothesis-based testing. Both are powerful approaches that allow you to get to the true causes of a problem. The 5-Whys method helps you peel back layers by repeatedly asking why until you uncover the root issue, rather than settling for surface-level symptoms. Hypothesis-based testing allows you to test assumptions and gather data to inform your understanding of the problem's causes.

The 5-Whys method

It's tempting to stop at the first explanation or the one that is easiest to find when searching for the cause of a problem. Often the real cause is lurking where you can't easily see it. The 5-Whys method forces you to look beyond what's obvious and systematically explore the chain of causes that led to the problem by asking why at least five times.

How it works

1. **Define your current situation**: Start with your description of the problem.
2. **Ask why**: Ask "Why did this happen?" and write down the answer.
3. **Repeat**: Take note of the answer and ask why again, digging deeper with each question.
4. **Continue until the root cause is found**: Repeat this process until you reach the root cause. It usually takes around five iterations.

There may be multiple causes contributing to the situation. Take note of all causes and the 5 Whys for each. This technique was drilled into me when I was a junior consultant. It helped make sure what I believed to be the true cause of a problem was grounded in facts.

Asking why until we find the cause of something is a tactic we're born with. If you've spent time with young child, you will have experienced them asking why all the time. It's how our brains seek to understand the real reason for something, so it can help us make sense of the world.

Don't be afraid to sound a bit like a young child repeatedly asking why. A little bit of effort will get you to the true cause of the problem and help you better understand the reason for it.

Hypothesis-based testing

If the 5-Whys method can't provide you with enough clarity on what's causing the problem, you will need to dig a little deeper. Hypothesis-based testing is your next option to get to root cause of your problem. Hypothesis-based testing is a structured method that involves developing and testing a hypothesis. A hypothesis is a possible explanation for a situation. There are four steps to performing a hypothesis-based test to determine the causes of a problem:

1. Develop your hypothesis.
2. Identify variables and metrics.
3. Gather data and test the hypothesis.
4. Analyse results and draw conclusions.

Develop your hypothesis

A hypothesis should be based on initial observations, available data, or knowledge about the problem's context. It's important that it be specific and actionable.

For instance, a hypothesis for a customer satisfaction problem could be: "Customer satisfaction scores have dropped because response times for customer inquiries have increased beyond our target of 24 hours".

This hypothesis focuses on a specific variable (response time) and suggests a causal relationship that can be tested. Design your hypothesis to balance the need for quick, cost-effective results and achieving a comprehensive understanding. Wherever you can, do more to gain greater clarity. The time and investment to understand the problem will return a hundredfold when it comes to developing solutions.

Identify variables and metrics

To test the hypothesis, identify the variables that you need to measure. These should relate directly to the hypothesis and provide insight into whether it holds true. In the example above, the variables could include average response time, volume of inquiries and customer satisfaction scores. Define the metrics for each variable, such as hours for response time and percentage points for satisfaction.

Gather data and test the hypothesis

Collect data that relates to the identified variables. This could involve analysing historical records, conducting surveys, or running controlled experiments. For the customer service example, you could gather data on response times and satisfaction scores over the past six months.

Next, look for patterns or correlations in the data. If the hypothesis is correct, you would expect to see a strong inverse correlation between response time and satisfaction scores, meaning as response times increased, satisfaction scores decreased.

Analyse results and draw conclusions

If the data supports the hypothesis, you have likely identified a contributing cause of the problem. For instance, if satisfaction scores dropped whenever response times exceeded 24 hours, this suggests that slow responses are a major factor.

If the data does not support the hypothesis, refine it or develop a new one based on additional information. You often need to test multiple hypotheses in sequence to get to the root causes.

ALISON'S PROBLEM

Alison arranged a meeting with Sandra from Sales to understand the reasons behind why they were being paid at 30 days and not 15 days. Alison decided to use the 5-Whys method to see if she could get to the bottom of it. When she met with Sandra, she asked her the following questions and received these responses:

Why 1: Why aren't we getting paid within 15 days?
Cause 1: Because our invoices say payment within 30 days.
Why 2: Why do invoices say payment in 30 days?
Cause 2: Because our contracts specify 30-day payment terms.
Why 3: Why do our contracts specify payment in 30 days?
Cause 3: Because it's an industry standard we've used for 10 years.
Why 4: Why did we choose to use an industry standard of 30 days?
Cause 4: Because we were new to the market 10 years ago and didn't feel we had the negotiating power to ask for better terms
Why 5: Why haven't we considered 15-day payment terms before now?
Cause 5: Because we hadn't thought of changing it as no one told us it was a problem until now.

Problem cause

Alison determined the most relevant cause of the problem was a consistent clause in all existing contracts specifying 30-day payment terms. This contract term has existed for the past 10 years.

Alison's next steps

Alison now felt she better understood the problem and how much it mattered to take action to solve it. She also felt confident she knew what was causing it. Alison understood the *reason* there was a problem and could move to the next step of choosing the specific result to aim for and if there were any constraints to be aware of when solving it.

CHAPTER 12

Understand the Reason

- The first step in in problem-solving is to understand the reason you have a problem by discovering its causes and whether it matters.
- A problem matters if it significantly impacts value, time, status or wellbeing.
- Finding the causes of a problem provides targets to develop your response to solve it.
- Causes of problems are often hidden from easy view. Use the 5-Whys method and hypothesis-based testing to discover the root causes of a problem if it's not obvious.

CHAPTER 13

Choose the Result

"First say to yourself what you would be, and then do what you have to do."
Epictetus

If you've already established that you're dealing with a problem that matters, one that's worth the time and energy to resolve, then it's time to move on to the next step: deciding what result you want to achieve and the conditions for success when you achieve it.

This is where problem-solving really starts to take shape. You've done the groundwork of understanding the challenging situation, its causes and why it's important to address it. Now you need to get specific about what success needs to look and feel like before you set off to find solutions that respond to the problem.

Combining the *reason* and the *result* you need forms your *problem definition*. This definition clarifies what the problem is, why it matters, and what success will be once it's solved. By establishing this definition and aligning it with key stakeholders, you'll create a smoother and more efficient path to finding a solution that works and adds the value you need.

Perhaps you're someone with action bias. If you are, you'll be building up a head of steam to begin making 'real' progress towards solving your problem. I'm one of these people too. I've had to learn that 'real' progress also means making sure I'm heading in the right direction. There is a time and place for solution-finding action, and that comes right after confirming your problem definition is the right one.

To choose the right result to aim for you need to:

1. **Specify what you need:** It's more than just saying, "I want to solve this". What exactly does solving it mean? Is it reducing costs by 10%? Is it delivering a new product within a certain timeframe? Is it closing the $20 million gap on revenue this year? The more precise you are, the better the solution you will develop.
2. **List the constraints:** Identify the limitations and exclusions you need to work with. This includes things like budget, time, resources and stakeholder concerns. Knowing these up front allows you to design a realistic and achievable solution that fits within the boundaries you must work with.

By taking the time to thoughtfully choose the result you want to achieve, you're not just solving a problem, you're setting yourself up to solve the *right* problem, in the *right* way. The clearer you are on what you need to achieve and the constraints you have to work with, the more confident you can be that your efforts will lead to the most valuable result.

Specify what you need

At first glance, deciding what result you need when solving a problem might seem straightforward. You identify the issue and then choose the outcome you believe will address it. Simple, right? Often, it's not so clear-cut. The best solutions to problems are found when the results you need are specific, pitched at the right level, aligned with influential stakeholders and use language that gives you the widest possible range of solutions to consider.

Be specific, be SMART

The first rule of choosing the right result is that it needs to be specific and directly related to the problem you're solving. It needs to be SMART: specific, measurable, action-oriented, relevant, time-bound and expressed as a need. For example, "We *need* customer payments of at least $200,000 to be paid within 15 days of invoice date each month starting in September".

The more specific you are, the more clearly you can communicate to others what you need to achieve and how they can help. Without this clarity, it's easy to veer off course or, worse, achieve a result that's ineffective or irrelevant.

Think of it this way: if you were navigating through dense fog, would you want to rely on vague directions, or would you prefer a GPS that clearly shows you the path and destination? The more clearly you can describe the result you need, the better your chances of navigating through the complexity of the problem and arriving at a solution that works.

Pitch your results at the right level

Do you aim for easy, do you aim for challenging, or do you aim for groundbreaking innovation and progress? Or are the results you need to achieve defined for you? This can be the case for legislative or other externally driven problems. The level at which you pitch the result you need, the goal you want to achieve, sets the level of tension and challenge when finding solutions. An easy goal is not motivating and can feel just like another task. A challenging and inspiring goal is motivating. An impossible goal creates stress and can immobilise people.

Where you have discretion to choose the result to aim for, consider carefully the short-term and long-term needs of the problem. As a minimum, align it with what your strategy and business plan require.

Always consider whether aiming higher will inspire and motivate, and never aim too low. Research has shown that people are often influenced by psychological biases and social pressures to set goals that are lower than what they could achieve.

There's a temptation to replace what has been lost with an equivalent or equal solution. This tendency, known as the 'status quo bias', is rooted in our psychological preference for familiarity and resistance to change. This bias leads us to settle for replacements that replicate what we've lost rather than considering more transformative options. There's a saying, "never waste a good crisis".

When you suffer a loss or need to replace what has stopped working, it can be an opportunity to move beyond the constraints of 'like-for-like' replacement. Consider a wider improvement that can deliver greater longer-term benefits than simply replacing what has been lost with an equivalent.

Bottom line: set your target result by aligning it with your organisation's strategy and business plan and ask yourself how you can do more, rather than how you can do less. You become more valuable by adding more value, not by limiting it.

Align stakeholders

If your problem needs the support of others in your organisation to solve it, you'll need to engage and align with them on the results that need to be achieved. Stakeholders, including colleagues, leaders and external parties with an interest in having your problem solved, will have a perspective on what they consider success to be. The level of interest and power stakeholders have dictates how much attention you need to give to them.

Set your result in consultation with stakeholders to the extent they have a significant impact or interest in the problem you are solving. Where you find opposing perspectives on what needs to be achieved, hold a meeting with all important stakeholders to discuss the problem and what needs to be achieved to understand all viewpoints and reach a consensus. If consensus can't be reached, the most senior person with accountability for the problem needs to make a call. You need alignment on what result to aim for before you start work on finding solutions. It wastes time and resources to do otherwise.

Use language that maximises your solution options

The language you use to describe the result you need to achieve has a significant bearing on what solutions are considered.

Limited language	**Broader language**
Our fridge is broken, *we need a new fridge.*	Our fridge is broken, *we need cold and frozen storage for our perishable food.*
We are hungry, *we need to cook a meal for us to eat tonight.*	We are hungry, *we need a meal for us to eat tonight.*

Define your result by the outcome you need, not by the solution you think might be most appropriate. Defining your result in language that limits potential solutions may be appropriate where you have insurmountable constraints. However, don't needlessly limit potential solutions by narrowly defining the result you need to achieve at the outset where you don't have to.

ALISON'S PROBLEM

Initial problem statement
We are currently being paid 30 days after invoice date, which is too slow. We need to be paid in 15 days or less starting in September, which is 90 days from now. This is a significant problem that affects our cash flow and the future of the business.

Problem cause
The cause of the problem is a consistent clause in all existing contracts, specifying 30-day payment terms. This contract term has existed for 10 years.

Further investigation

Alison discussed the problem further with Jim, the Financial Controller, and asked, "What is the minimum financial amount that needs to be paid by customers within 15 days?" She needed to know what result would be acceptable in financial terms. Jim ran some analysis for her and once it was complete said, "We need a minimum of $2,000,000 in customer payments to be made within 15 days of invoice date".

She also wondered for how long the result had to last, so she asked Jim, "How long do we need this solution to last? Is this a short-term fix or a permanent fix?" Jim replied, "We need this in place for at least the next two years".

Ideal result

Alison determined the ideal result to aim for was to receive $2,000,000 of customer payments within 15 days of invoice date each month, starting within 90 days and continuing for at least two years.

Revised problem statement

She revised her problem statement to be:

We are currently being paid 30 days after invoice date, which is too slow. We need to receive at least $2,000,000 of customer payments within 15 days of invoice date, starting in September, and to have these earlier payments continue for at least the next two years to improve our cash flow.

List the constraints

Constraints are limitations that provide the parameters within which a problem needs to be solved. They can take various forms, such as financial restrictions, technical limitations, regulatory requirements or even tight deadlines.

Constraints serve to focus and channel creativity, pushing people and teams to devise novel solutions that might not have been considered under more comfortable circumstances. Jeff Bezos said, "Frugality drives innovation, just like other constraints do. One of the only ways to get out of a tight box is to invent your way out."

At first glance, constraints might seem like barriers to progress, stifling creativity and limiting possibilities. However, there are many studies that have proved that constraints improve creativity and innovation.[29]

> **The result you aim for needs to be specific and directly related to the problem you're solving.**

Constraints help focus the mind on overcoming limitations, which spurs creativity and innovation.

When developing the original Macintosh computer and faced with limited resources, Steve Jobs enforced a constraint that the Macintosh team could only use a specific amount of memory chips in the computer. This limitation led the team to explore innovative ways of designing software and hardware to optimise the use of those limited resources. The result was a breakthrough product that revolutionised personal computing.

Guitarist Eddie Van Halen from American rock band Van Halen developed his distinctive tapping and harmonic playing style because he couldn't afford equipment such as a fuzz box or wah-wah pedals to create the sounds he wanted. This constraint helped him become one of the all-time great rock guitarists.

Dr Seuss wrote the famous children's book *The Cat in the Hat* with only 236 different words. His editor challenged him to write a book with only 50 different words. Dr Seuss met the challenge with his book *Green Eggs and Ham*, one of the bestselling children's books of all time.

When there are no constraints on the creative process, complacency tends to set in. Psychologists call it following the path of least resistance, where people choose an idea that's intuitive and easy rather than investing in the development of better ideas because there is no reason not to do otherwise.[30]

There are three types of constraints to consider:

1. **Input constraints**
   Input constraints are limitations on the resources or conditions required to develop and implement a solution These include time, information, human capital, financial resources, asset availability, system limitations, values, and available materials.
2. **Process constraints**
   A process constraint is a limitation or restriction within the method or steps used to develop and implement a solution. These include guidelines on how teams should interact (such as in-person or virtually), which parts of the organisation and external parties to involve, testing rules, level of disruption to daily work, capacity of equipment being used and geographic limitations.
3. **Output constraints**
   An output constraint is a limitation, expectation or restriction on the results or outcomes that need to be achieved by a given solution. These include specifications that need to be achieved to solve the problem. Examples include quality measures, sales performance, regulatory compliance, customer feedback, staff survey results, financial requirements, and acquisition of new assets, capabilities or technology.

Some constraints are discretionary, meaning you can choose to include them or not. Others you are forced to include, and these are non-discretionary. These are 'must haves' or 'must nots'. For example, you might have to include using a particular supplier or software system, or you can only work at night.

Balancing constraints

When setting constraints for the problem you're solving, be mindful of the balance between motivation and overwhelm. Where the space to create novel ideas and explore possibilities is too tight, it can quickly kill creativity and become a drain on motivation.

A typical problem to solve should contain tight output constraints (which is the result you need), moderate input constraints (such as time to complete the project and available funds) and wide freedom in terms of the process through which the team develops solutions.

The Yerkes–Dodson Law, developed in 1908 by psychologists Robert M. Yerkes and John Dillingham Dodson, suggests that performance peaks with a healthy level of pressure, but there's a sweet spot. Too little tension and people lose motivation. Too much, and it leads to stress that can cripple decision-making. This balance is crucial when setting constraints to solve a problem.

> **Constraints help focus the mind on overcoming limitations, which spurs creativity and innovation.**

The key is to establish realistic yet challenging boundaries. To set the right balance of constraints and creative freedom, consider the nature of the problem and the amount of innovation that's required to be successful. The more innovation needed, the more the team will benefit from well-defined output constraints to focus on and relaxing input and process constraints so there's flexibility to test and explore ideas to create novel solutions.

Where innovation required is more moderate, such as moving office locations or rebranding a website, having tighter input and process constraints along with specific output requirements to manage time and cost in balance with outcomes will generate the best results.

Problem definition checklist

You're now ready to finalise your problem definition. Use the following checklist to confirm your problem definition is properly structured and described to maximise the potential solutions you discover.

- Is it expressed as a need that requires a solution?
- Is it focused on the most important issue?
- Does it clearly describe the current situation and its causes?
- Is it aligned with strategies and business plans?
- Does it include a specific and measurable outcome?
- Does it provide clear and compelling implications of inaction?
- Does it incorporate appropriate constraints?
- Does it include a deadline if time is critical?
- Have key stakeholder expectations been sufficiently considered?

ALISON'S PROBLEM

Problem statement

We are currently being paid 30 days after invoice date, which is too slow. We need to receive at least $2,000,000 of customer payments within 15 days of invoice date, starting in September, and have these earlier payments continue for at least the next two years to improve our cash flow.

Problem cause

The cause of the problem is a consistent clause in all existing contracts specifying 30-day payment terms, which has existed for the past 10 years.

Further investigation

Alison wondered if there were any other constraints that were important to consider when developing options to solve the problem. She asked Jim, the Financial Controller, if he could think of any. Jim told her, "The solution needs to be very reliable, meaning we need $2,000,000 to be paid consistently within 15 days of invoice date each month, not $50,000 one month and $2,000,000 the next".

He also said the maximum cost of the solution should be 5% of invoice value and that other banking arrangements could not be used.

She wondered if the sales team might have any constraints, so she called Sandra and asked for her thoughts. Sandra said, "There can be little to no impact on customer relationships".

Alison now had enough information to develop an initial list of constraints she could work with.

Additional constraints

Certainty – we need to be 100% certain of the $2,000,000 being paid within 15 days every month.

Disruption – we want limited impact to customers in the short term.

Cost – we are willing to pay a discount or fee of up to 5% of invoice value to bring the cash flow forward to 15 days payment.

Banking – we can't increase the limits or modify existing financial loans and facilities.

Next steps

Alison felt she had enough to go back to Jessie to confirm she understood the problem and the result she would need to deliver. She revised her problem definition using the Problem Definition Worksheet and sent it in an email to Jessie asking for feedback and approval to proceed.

Jessie confirmed in a return email. "Yes that's exactly what the problem is and the result I want. Be careful with the banks. Good luck finding solutions for us to consider I look forward to hearing the options you develop!"

PROBLEM DEFINITION WORKSHEET

Core need (problem statement)

Describe the core need that must be fulfilled. It must be specific, focused on the core issue, infer a specific outcome, provide implications and include a deadline if this is critical to success.

(We are currently being paid 30 days after invoice date, which is too slow. We need to receive at least $2,000,000 of customer payments within 15 days of invoice date starting in September and have this continue for at least the next two years to improve our cash flow.)

Why it matters	Primary causes/hypothesis
List the most critical current or future impacts of the problem remaining unresolved. Include impacts to value, status, time or wellbeing. Be specific. Link to strategy or business plan success. *(Cash flow is forecast to be critically tight in the next two years.)*	List primary causes that contribute to the problem and its perpetuation or the best hypothesis you have that needs testing. *(Current contracts specify 30-day payment terms and have done so for the past 10 years. No attempts at earlier payment have been made until now.)*

Conditions for success	Constraints
Define what must be achieved to consider solving the problem a success. Include qualitative and quantitative measures. Must be endorsed by stakeholders. *(Minimum of $2,000,000 customer payments each month paid within 15 days of invoice date. Early payments to commence by September, which is in 90 days, and continue for two years.)*	List what must be observed or must not be disturbed or included when solving the problem and implementing a solution. *(Certainty of payment amounts and timing, limited customer disruption, willing to pay up to 5% discount, no increase or amendments to current banking facilities, customer contracts renew on a rolling basis every two years.)*

Stakeholders

List the key stakeholders who are critical to engage with and the status of your engagement.

(Jessie, CEO—sponsor; Jim, Financial Controller—financial constraints and banking relationship; Sandra, Head of Sales—customer insight and relationships. All stakeholders have been engaged. Jim and Sandra are aligned with this problem definition and now seeking endorsement from Jessie.)

CHAPTER 13

Choose the RESULT

- Time invested to choose the right results to achieve sets you up to solve the *right* problem, in the *right* way.
- Be specific and pitch your results at the right level. Never aim too low.
- Define results using language that will give you the widest range of potential solutions to consider.
- Don't set results without constraints. They are essential to unlocking creativity and fuelling motivation.

CHAPTER 14

Develop the Response (Part 1)

"The true delight is in the finding out, rather than in the knowing."
Isaac Asimov

In this last step of the problem-solving process, you get to be creative, collaborative and, most of all, feel the satisfaction of solving your problem. You now know you have a *reason* to take action to solve a problem that matters, and you know the *result* you need to achieve. So, it's now time to get to work and take some action to develop and select the right *response*.

This is where positivity, perseverance and patience become your most important assets. Developing solutions to challenging problems can take time and involve experimentation, pushing against boundaries and learning from setbacks. This is also where the most development and new learning comes from. It's where you shift from *observing* problems to *solving* them. I've split this step into two parts to make it easier for you to work your way through. This chapter focuses on the first three actions and Chapter 15 focuses on the last two.

To develop a response to solve a problem you need to:

1. Recruit the right support.
2. List causes as opportunities.
3. Identify options.
4. Maximise the result (see Chapter 15).
5. Plan and implement the solution (see Chapter 15).

Recruit the right support

When tackling a problem that requires collaboration, identifying and recruiting the right team members is essential. The people you choose to work with can significantly impact not only the effectiveness of your solutions, but also the dynamics of the problem-solving process itself. Every problem comes with its own set of challenges and timelines, often demanding a diverse range of skills and experiences. Much like selecting a boating crew, the right crew composition varies depending on the nature of the trip and the conditions. Your crew will be different if you're captaining a container ship and sailing across the ocean or piloting a passenger ferry from one domestic port to another.

When choosing people to work with, consider these four questions. I call them the Core Four team attributes.

1. Do they have the **Capability** to perform what's required of them?
2. Do they have the **Influence** or **Authority** to capture the attention and cooperation of stakeholders?
3. Do they have the **Capacity** to complete the work you need them to?
4. Do they have the **Desire** to work with you and the wider team to solve the problem?

The best people you can select to work with are the ones that you can say "Hell yes!" to each of these questions.

Capability

Start by defining what you need people to do and group these into roles that people can fill. List the specific expertise, outcomes and deliverables required for the problem at hand. Do you need someone to lead a team, provide analytical insights, effectively communicate with stakeholders, or collaborate on innovative solutions?

Also identify the inherent qualities necessary for success in the role. Do they need to be a creative thinker capable of generating fresh ideas? Do they need strong communication skills to convey complex information concisely and simply? Clearly articulating these needs will help ensure that you find people who can truly contribute to solving the problem.

Influence

Solving problems delivers change and often relies heavily on collaboration and communication with others to be successful. It also relies on access to resources and knowledge. The ability to influence stakeholders and gain their support is vital. Consider who the person needs to be able to successfully influence and work with and what specific resources they must be able to access to be effective on the team, and whether they can provide these.

Capacity

Contributing to solving problems in the beginning may require limited time investment. However, this can change dramatically where there's commitment to implement a solution. As best you can, be clear on the expected time commitment required of someone before you begin searching to fill a role. If you're not certain of the exact time commitment, provide the best estimate you can.

Teams perform at their best when there is trust between members. Trust is created when people spend time together and form a bond to achieve a goal. When people change frequently, it takes time to rebuild trust and recapture lost momentum.

Think of it like this: if your sailing trip was to take three months and your crew member only had one month available, that wouldn't work so well, would it?

Desire

This is the attribute that can make or break solving a problem more than any other. Someone can have the right capability, influence and capacity, but without the motivation to solve the problem, they will struggle to be successful.

I once led a team to create a new process and technology solution to induct new contactors into a large construction business. The existing process was expensive to administer because it was manual, and it frustrated contractors because it was overly time-consuming and error-prone. Recruiting for team members, someone I trusted recommended a person with vast knowledge and experience in the problem I had to solve. When I initially spoke with him, he expressed his interest and willingness to help contribute to a solution to the problem. He said he had capacity for a day a week for two months, which worked well.

However, two weeks into our work, cracks started to appear. My highly recommended resource stopped doing the work that was assigned to him, didn't turn up to meetings, and virtually vanished. His reason, "It wasn't critical to me to do this and my other work, and I've gotten busy so can't help you anymore".

There was no consequence for him in dropping out of the work he had committed to support me on. He didn't think it was 'his problem'. No ownership means no real commitment. Work with people who are committed to being part of solving an important problem and who clear a path to create time to support you. They provide energy and ideas, and stay with you to make things happen. Where someone is reluctantly involved, it can feel like an anchor pulling against the rest of the team.

Ask the person you are considering involving what excites them about the problem. What part of it motivates them to help solve it? A problem that needs significant challenges to be overcome over a long period of time will need considerable discretionary effort. Make sure there is something meaningful in it for the person you're considering asking to help you. It could be part of their career progression, learning new skills or the chance to achieve something significant. Or, if they are an external expert, it could be the opportunity to work with you and get to know your business.

If you can't say "Hell yes!" to each of these Core Four team attribute questions, then the answer is they are not a good fit for your team. Keep looking. You will find the right person. It's not just about getting anyone to help you, it's about having the right people in the right roles. If they aren't right, you know they are the wrong people to help you.

ALISON'S PROBLEM

Problem statement
We are currently being paid 30 days after invoice date, which is too slow. We need to receive at least $2,000,000 of customer payments within 15 days of invoice date starting in September and have this continue for at least the next two years to improve our cash flow.

Further investigation
Alison knew enough about the problem and how it affected the business now to understand the skills and type of people she needed to work with to help her find a solution. A small team of experienced and committed people should be able to find a solution.

Because there was such a short timeframe to develop and implement a solution, less than 90 days, the people she needed to work with must have the capacity to work within her timelines. There was also no straightforward solution, so the team would need to do some exploring, idea generation and collaboration to find and implement a solution.

Alison decided to find a person from each of the following parts of the business to help:

Sales

They have the customer relationships and know the details of their contracts. Their help in understanding the impact of the options being considered on customers would be useful too.

Operations

They may have ideas on how changes to processes or systems could add to the speed and practicality of implementing a solution.

Finance

While they can't use existing financial facilities, maybe there are other ideas that could be used as part of a solution. It was a long-shot idea, but Alison thought it was worth including someone who at least knew about the current finance arrangements.

Legal

If customer contracts need to be changed or other arrangements entered into, someone from legal would be helpful to identify ideas for that and connect the team to other people who could help.

Before she set off to ask each department for help, Alison decided it would be a great idea to confirm with her boss that this list of skills would be good to start with. Her boss agreed and offered to call the heads of each area to ask for help and to await Alison's call.

Alison now had the Core Four team attribute questions and developed a recruiting checklist with questions to help her find the right kind of people when she met with the heads of each department. She now felt confident she could find people who were willing and able to help her.

List causes as opportunities

Here's where the detective work you've completed, uncovering the causes of the problem, provides the springboard to launch creative thinking and ideas on how to solve it. You're now standing on the starting line of what will be an exhilarating ride from unknowing to knowing.

Creativity wakes up when you start asking questions. Questions focus the mind to find an answer or search for an idea or a person that could lead to an answer. They create momentum and spark new ideas. They connect you closer to the result you want to achieve.

To provide focus for your creative thinking, list the causes of the problem you are trying to solve then reframe them as questions. This turns the causes of a problem into opportunities and opens your mind to search for ideas and solutions. It's shifting from 'why' to 'how'. 'Why' is backward looking, whereas 'how' focuses on the future. Finding solutions means looking forward.

Another reason to switch to using 'how' is it removes any further judgement or blame for what caused the problem, which can divide teams and undermine progress. Using 'how' aligns people to find a solution which brings them together.

Reframing the causes of problems into opportunities shifts your perspective from focusing on what you lack to what you can gain. As Carl Jung put it, "To ask the right question is already half the solution to a problem". Changing the cause of a problem into a question that asks how it can be overcome is the right question to ask.

For example
Cause: Raw material suppliers are not delivering on time, causing delays in our production.
Opportunity: How can we maintain production even when raw material deliveries are delayed?
Cause: Our pricing is now above our competitors', and we are losing sales.
Opportunity: How can we enhance the value we offer to customers compared to our competitors to increase sales?
Cause: We are manually entering information into our database, which is creating errors and consuming too much time and cost.

Opportunity: How can we improve the transfer of information into our database to increase speed and reliability and reduce cost?

ALISON'S PROBLEM

Problem statement

We are currently being paid 30 days after invoice date, which is too slow. We need to receive at least $2,000,000 of customer payments within 15 days of invoice date starting in September, and have this continue for at least the next two years to improve our cash flow.

Further investigation

Alison called her new team together for their first workshop: Phil from Finance, Sandra from Sales, Jimmy from Operations and Sally from legal.

Alison explained the problem, the ideal result they needed to achieve and the constraints they needed to work with. She wrote the causes of the problem on the whiteboard and reframed each as opportunities.

Cause	Opportunity
Our contracts specify payment terms of 30 days when we now want to be paid in 15 days.	How do we change or work around current contract payment terms of 30 days to get paid in 15 days?
Contract terms are an industry standard that haven't changed in 10 years.	How do we influence a change to the current payment term standard so we don't have to stick with them in the future?

Alison gave the team 10 minutes to come up with ideas before they would discuss them as a group.

Identify options

Identifying options is finding and connecting dots or pieces of a puzzle to create a picture that you like; a picture that solves the problem. You can see or find some pieces easily, and others you need to work to discover. The temptation is to rush to find a solution to avoid feeling uncertain about what to do. Resist this urge. Instead, find comfort in following a process and trusting your judgement to lead you to the solution you need.

Start developing your options by asking two questions that address the causes of the problem. Make sure you examine each cause and find solutions for each. It may be that one solution may address multiple causes.

1. What can I change that I currently do? (start, stop, do more or do less of).
2. What can I change that I currently have? (move, remove, develop or acquire).

If you have a team, facilitate a discussion to generate options, or use more creative methods described below including hero switching, starbursting, and Edward de Bono's PMI method.

What can I change that I currently do?

Start doing something

What new process, protocol, restriction, service, training or method could be introduced that would address the causes of the problem and help you achieve what you need? What combination of new and old could lead to a breakthrough? What new steps could be added, or different combinations of actions could alleviate the causes of the problem?

Stop doing something

What can be stopped entirely? How would this affect other parts of the problem in positive and negative ways? Can the negatives be offset elsewhere or tolerated as a consequence of solving the problem? Can you stop a service, cease a product feature, no longer require something that was once considered essential, or swap something out for a better alternative?

Do more of something

What is working well but could be accelerated, boosted or made larger in its application that would solve the problem? How could that be achieved? For example, more training, extended opening hours, increased marketing spending, or faster delivery and production times. What enhanced features or services can be added?

Do less of something

What could be reduced in its timing, frequency, use, intensity or location that would solve the problem? How could you take less time, remove steps, reduce waste, reduce hand-offs or use less of? If you currently *do* something for others, what can you change so they *do it with you* or *do it by themselves* that will solve your problem?

What can I change that I currently have?

Move what you have

What do you have that's causing or being affected by the problem that could be moved to a new location? How can you relocate people, digital or physical assets, venues, meetings, events or services from where or when they are performed to somewhere different?

Remove what you have

What could be removed or replaced entirely to solve the problem? "Possibly the most common error of a smart engineer is to optimise a thing that should not exist", says Elon Musk.

Develop something new

What new equipment, technology, intellectual property or other asset could be developed by you or in partnership with others that would solve the problem? For example, developing biodegradable plastic bags to replace petrochemical-based plastic bags.

Acquire something new
What new equipment, technology, services or other capability could be acquired by you from a third party or another part of the organisation that could solve the problem? What can be borrowed or loaned to get you started? What new information, research or experience can be gained to bring new perspectives on the problem?

The ideas you generate in response to these questions become the ingredients for options to test and evaluate. Continue considering solutions to address the causes of your problem until you run out of ideas. Be methodical. Don't assume the first idea will be the best.

Strategies to help generate ideas

When ideas to solve a problem are limited or new thinking is needed to uncover options not yet considered, you may need to get a little creative in how you find ideas to work with. Below are five techniques to consider if you find yourself in this situation.

Solo brainstorming
The general principle of this technique is to separate generating ideas from discussing them.

If you have a team available, the leader of the team presents the problem, its causes and constraints, but not the ideas already considered. Team members write down their ideas, initially without collaborating. This helps eliminate anchoring bias and encourages everyone to develop their own ideas. It also gives people more time to think over their ideas, which is especially helpful for introverted participants.

This technique works best for teams who may be heavily influenced by either the first ideas presented or by an influential person in the meeting.

Once you have your collection of individually crafted ideas, the team leader can write them on a whiteboard without attribution. The merits of each will be discussed without disclosing the author.

Hero switching

This is where you shift your thinking from yourself and imagine what someone you admire greatly would want to do.

Have you ever considered how someone else might solve a problem? Or what they might say about a particular situation? With hero switching, your aim is to do just that.

Think about how someone like your boss, or a famous person like Steve Jobs or Elon Musk, might consider the problem you need to solve. By putting yourself in other people's shoes, imagining how their mind works and how they might view your situation can generate new ideas from which new possibilities can spring. This technique works best when you or your team are feeling low on energy or are feeling a bit stale from progressive waves of problems that need solving.

Starbursting

This technique focuses on using questions rather than answers to generate ideas. Starbursting is where you or your team are challenged to list as many questions as you can to find alternative ways of looking at the problem to see if that generates new ideas.

Cover the six essential questions of who, what, why, when, where and how. Each point of the star represents one of these questions. The idea is to brainstorm as many relevant questions as possible in each category to deeply explore a problem or situation. The emphasis is on understanding all aspects before jumping to solutions, helping to uncover hidden challenges, details and opportunities.

A good focus for starbursting is to use inversion, where you restate the problem from the opposite perspective to see if it sparks ideas. See Chapter 17 *Choose the Opposite Way* for details on how to use inversion as a problem-solving strategy.

Stepladder

This technique encourages every member of the team to contribute before being influenced by others. It's a variation of solo brainstorming, but with progressive collaboration added in.

Start by sharing the topic to be considered. Everyone leaves the room after the topic is shared, with the exception of two team members. These two people discuss the topic and their ideas and once they have concluded their discussion, one more person will join the room to contribute their ideas. The new ideas are to be discussed by the three people before the ideas discussed between the original two people.

Repeat this cycle until all members of the team have contributed their ideas. One of the original two team members takes charge of recording the new ideas and any iterations developed during discussion. This is a great technique to avoid the perils of unconscious group think.

Outsider peer perspective

When our minds are full of the details of a problem, it can often become overwhelming to pull ourselves out to see it from alternative perspectives. Inviting a person or a group of people to share their ideas and thoughts without constraint can help provide moments if inspiration that can move a problem from quicksand to skating downhill.

To do this, select a group of people who are knowledgeable about parts of your problem as well as people who have little to no domain expertise. Widen the lens of potential new perspectives as far as you need to, to generate new ideas.

Provide the peer group with a short briefing document about the problem, your ideal result, and any constraints. This is a great way to use experts without having to commit to a specific solution they provide. Don't share the ideas of the peer group at this point. Let the creativity flow individually. Bring the peer group together to discuss their ideas in a workshop and use them to find potential new angles, ideas or avenues of inquiry to open up new options.

Pluses, minuses and what's interesting (PMI)

It's common to think only in binary terms when an idea is presented; to think of what's good and what's bad about it. It's how pros and cons are typically formed when we consider ideas. But this type of thinking can prematurely kill off potentially great ideas because we don't know enough about them to judge them fairly or see where the idea could be valuable if combined with another idea.

Ideas often need help to develop into viable solutions. Mark Zuckerberg observed, "Ideas don't come out fully formed. They only become clear as you work on them".

To counteract this limitation in thinking, Edward de Bono developed the PMI model. When an idea is created and shared, instead of just asking what its pluses and minuses are, also ask what's interesting about it. Asking a neutral question about the idea provides the opportunity to build on it rather than judge it as good or bad, to be kept or disposed of.

For example

- **Idea:** Switch all product packaging to fully biodegradable materials to align with our values.
- **Positives:** Reduces environmental impact and positions the company as a leader in sustainability, attracts environmentally conscious consumers, potentially increasing market share, and lowers long-term costs associated with waste disposal and regulatory compliance.
- **Negatives:** Higher production costs compared to conventional packaging, potential compromise on durability or shelf life of the product, and limited suppliers and uncertain supply chain stability.

- **Interesting:** Could we partner with suppliers to co-develop a cost-effective biodegradable material that addresses durability issues? What if we launched a campaign inviting customers to submit their packaging ideas, fostering community engagement and brand loyalty? Could we incorporate technology like QR codes or sensors in the packaging to educate customers on disposal methods, recycling, or environmental impact?

What's interesting could then be further explored. Could partnering with suppliers lead to the creation of a new biodegradable material, not only solving the company's issue but also providing a potential new product line for the supplier? Would crowdsourcing ideas from customers reveal creative packaging concepts that haven't been considered internally, and lead to customers feeling more connected to the brand? Would integrating technology into packaging position the brand as innovative and tech-savvy while providing added value through education, enhancing the overall customer experience?

Exploring the interesting aspects of an idea can reveal new paths and solutions that wouldn't be visible through a standard pros and cons evaluation. This approach encourages creative thinking and can help refine and expand on initial ideas to develop breakthrough innovations.

Crowdsource ideas

Crowdsourcing is low-cost and fast way to leverage the collective intelligence and creativity of a large group of people to generate ideas and solve problems. By tapping into a wider pool of diverse perspectives and backgrounds, you can quickly gain insights that might not emerge in traditional brainstorming settings.

Take these steps to use crowdsourcing as an idea generation strategy:

1. **Select the platform to use:**
    - **Internal group chats:** platforms such as Slack or Microsoft Teams provide a simple and cost-effective way of seeking input from a wide internal crowd.
    - **Crowdsourcing software platforms:** your organisation may have crowdsourcing software, such as BrightIdea, which makes crowdsourcing ideas a richer and more in-depth experience.
2. **Post your request:** Share your problem as you've defined it so far and ask a specific question you want help exploring. Be specific, as this helps focus your crowd on how they can help and makes later analysis much easier.
3. **Engage the crowd:** through your company social media, email or community channels. Encourage participation by making it accessible and inviting. Offer an incentive (if appropriate) for the ideas that contribute most to a solution.
4. **Collect ideas**: Allow participants to submit their ideas and suggestions within a timeframe.
5. **Facilitate discussion**: Encourage interaction among participants to refine ideas. This can include comment threads, polls or forums.
6. **Group ideas for consideration:** Filter ideas into themes and feed into your next team discussion.
7. **Provide feedback:** showcase how the crowdsourcing process benefited your problem-solving process by sharing a post afterwards. Showing gratitude and providing insights to others will contribute to a culture of supportive problem-solving.

Explore knowledge gaps and challenge assumptions

Understanding what you *don't* know is just as important as understanding what you *do* know. But how do you find out what you don't know? It starts with knowing that you can't possibly have perfect information and putting safeguards in place to ask questions of the information and the assumptions you have to *actively* decide if you need more.

Research has found we have a hidden bias in our brains that makes us assume we have all the information we need to make choices, without considering the key details we *don't* have.[31]

Psychologists call this the 'illusion of information adequacy', and it's a paradox that plagues problem-solving. In theory, we know we don't know everything, and yet we often behave as if we have all the right information to back up our opinions, decisions and judgements.

A study involving 1,261 participants asked them to decide whether to merge two schools or keep them separate. Some participants received all the pros and cons of merging, while others were only given either the pros or the cons. None of the participants were aware they were missing information.

As expected, those who only received pro-merging details recommended the schools merge, and those with only pro-separation details suggested keeping them separate. The surprising part? Those with partial information believed they were just as informed and capable of making a decision as anyone else. In fact, the participants who had only half the story felt more confident in their decision than those who had all the facts.

The study showed how people often don't realise when they're operating from an incomplete perspective. To avoid succumbing to this bias ask, "What don't we yet know?" and "What assumptions have we made that we need to test?" before you exhaust identifying solution options.

Don't let fear subconsciously limit your creativity

Fear significantly limits developing solution options. Research by consultants McKinsey has found there are three fears that limit creativity and innovation more than any others: fear of criticism, fear of uncertainty, and fear of a negative impact on someone's career.[32]

The fear of career impact was found to have the greatest effect on innovative thinking and progress. When you fear for your role, loss aversion becomes your key motivator. You will be more biased to look for safe and predictable options and discount considering higher-risk options.

The fear of losing control was found to have the next most significant impact. When we fear losing control, we subconsciously favour options with more predictable outcomes and discount ones with higher uncertainty but that have potentially greater results.

Fearing criticism is common. If you are part of a team, fitting in and being part of the 'tribe' is often seen as important to your success. However, too much fear means options that could break with tradition or go against established norms will either not be raised or will be discounted quickly, even if they show potential.

If you think there may be fears undermining your team's creativity, consider these interventions to counteract them.

Discuss and neutralise

Have a conversation with your team about how fear can impact creativity. Ask team members to list the fears they have or can see and rate them based on the perceived impact on creativity. Use a scale of one to 10, with the highest score meaning the greatest impact on creativity. If you suspect fear is high, make team members' contributions anonymous. Where a fear is rated more than five on average, it should be addressed.

Use the framework acknowledge—discuss—root causes—solutions. Fears are to be expected when solving challenging problems. Fears that are left to grow become invisible barriers that prevent progress.

Look for signs

Be on the lookout for signs you are letting fear take the wheel. If you or your team are jumping for easy solutions or arguing against options that go against norms but would create better results, call a meeting to discuss your observations and raise awareness.

Ask for support

Words of support from someone in a senior role may alleviate specific fears, particularly the fear of failure and impact on careers.

Create a fear free moment

Ask yourself or your team to put themselves in a mindset of 'failure cannot happen'. Say, "Assume anything we did will work out, no matter what. Now, what can you think of that we could do?" This helps you let go of fear as a handbrake on your thinking and creativity.

Package up your options

Time now to start packaging. By that I mean grouping your potential solutions to the causes of your problem into distinct packages to evaluate and choose from. Creating distinct options makes it easier to decide what action to take to solve your problem. By grouping solutions into packages that tackle the underlying causes of your problem, you can step back and assess each potential path based on its advantages, risks and possible outcomes. It ensures you're not merely addressing individual causes, but are focused on finding the most effective way to resolve the problem as a whole. Here's how to do it.

Identify core themes or categories

Start by reviewing all the potential solutions to the causes of the problem and look for commonalities. Group the solutions based on shared characteristics, such as:

- **Method**: Do the solutions involve similar methods, like technology upgrades, process changes or type of equipment?
- **Scope**: Is there a larger scale solution and other more moderate scope options?
- **Cost**: Are they budget-friendly, moderate, or expensive?
- **Resources**: Is there a difference in the type and nature of resources, for example onshoring vs offshoring?
- **Timeline**: Are these quick wins or longer-term investments?

Group by cause or issue

Another way to group solutions is by the specific causes of the problem they address. For example, if a problem has been broken down into categories like process, people, tools and environment, you can categorise solutions according to which of these root causes they aim to resolve.

- **Process-based solutions:** Streamlining workflows or reducing redundancies.
- **People-based solutions:** Training or reassigning staff.
- **Tool-based solutions:** Upgrading software or equipment.
- **Environment-based solutions:** Changing workplace layout or improving communication channels.

Combine similar solutions

Look for individual solutions that can be combined into broader options. For example, if multiple solutions involve improving communication, you could group them into a single option, such as 'Revamp internal communication channels'.

Present as distinct options

Finally, present the grouped solutions as distinct options. For example:
- **Option 1: Process re-engineering:**
  Focus on simplifying processes and improving workflows.
- **Option 2: Technology investment:**
  Invest in new tools and systems to improve efficiency.
- **Option 3: Training and development:**
  Provide staff with more training and support.

Example

Imagine a startup facing delays in product delivery. The individual solutions could be:
- Automating part of the assembly process
- Hiring additional workers for peak times
- Changing the supply chain provider

These could be grouped into distinct options:
- **Option 1: Automation focus:**
  Automate processes to reduce human error and speed up production.
- **Option 2: Workforce expansion:**
  Increase staff during peak periods to keep up with demand.
- **Option 3: Supply chain overhaul:**
  Optimise or change suppliers to improve lead times.

By organising solutions into options, you create clear pathways for evaluation and decision-making.

ALISON'S PROBLEM

Problem statement

We are currently being paid 30 days after invoice date, which is too slow. We need to receive at least $2,000,000 of customer payments within 15 days of invoice date starting in September and have this continue for at least the next two years to improve our cash flow.

Further investigation

Alison and her team worked through each of the two sets of four option possibilities to list what they thought were ideas to consider. No ideas were to be evaluated until all ideas had been identified.

Sandra suggested they could offer an incentive to customers if they paid in 15 days instead of 30 days.

Sally suggested they could open negotiations to revise customer contracts with enough sales volume to achieve $2,000,000 payments within 15 days.

The team fell flat for a minute. No obvious solution was jumping out at them. Alison wondered if something could be found by using the problem-solving tactic *inversion*— where you reverse the problem and see what ideas pop out.

Alison wrote on the whiteboard in their meeting room: We want to be paid by our customers in 15 days. She highlighted our customers and asked the team, "What if we weren't paid by our customers but by someone else?"

That sparked an idea in Jimmy's mind. "I remember a conversation with a friend of mine about some of their suppliers using a finance company to be paid earlier than my friend's company would pay them. I hadn't thought of it until you said, 'paid by someone else'", he said.

Jimmy called his friend who gave him the name of the finance company he had mentioned. Jimmy called the company and found out details of how a debtor finance arrangement could work, the application process, and approximate costs and timeframes to implement.

Based on that conversation, Jimmy said it would be possible to have a debtor finance facility in place within 90 days, but at a cost of 6% of invoice value plus a one-off establishment fee. Customers would need to be notified of the debtor finance arrangement, but it didn't seem like a difficult process to set up.

Phil called Jim, the Financial Controller, and confirmed that debtor financing would be an acceptable solution and would not interfere with other financing arrangements.

The team now had three options to consider.

Customer early payment incentive

Offer an incentive of up to 5% discount to customers if they pay in 15 days instead of 30 days.

Renegotiate customer contracts

Open negotiations with customers to revise contracts to have payment terms of 15 days not 30 days.

Secure debtor financing

Secure a debtor financing facility from a finance company, where they pay within 15 days of invoices provided to them.

CHAPTER 14

Develop the Response (Part 1)

- The optimal response to a problem is the one that gets closest to achieving the desired result and addresses its root causes within the constraints you have.
- Select team members to support you based on their capability, influence, capacity, and desire to collaborate in solving the problem.
- Switch the causes of a problem into questions to stimulate curiosity and creativity to find solutions.
- Consider changing what you do, changing what you have, or a combination of both to create solution options.
- Generate new ideas by using inversion, solo brainstorming, hero switching, starbursting, crowdsourcing, outsider peer perspectives and PMI techniques.

CHAPTER 15

Develop the Response (Part 2)

"In any moment of decision, the best thing you can do is the right thing, the next best thing is the wrong thing, and the worst thing you can do is nothing."
Theodore Roosevelt

What's left is to decide what to do and get to work to do it. You've defined the problem, have a clear result in mind and have developed multiple options to choose from. In many cases, the best option to select will be relatively straightforward.

But for complex problems with options that are highly contrasted, span multiple time horizons or have varying degrees of certainty attached to them, deciding what is the 'best' response takes some careful thought. It's where many of the cognitive biases that cause thinking traps listed in Chapter 10 appear. Biases such as the bandwagon effect, the certainty effect, confirmation bias, loss aversion, the framing effect and the sunk cost fallacy can rear their ugly heads during this penultimate part of the problem-solving process. Be on the lookout for them to make sure you and your team select the most appropriate response that maximises your result.

The last two actions to develop your response are:

1. Maximise the result.
2. Plan and implement the solution.

Maximise the result

Maximising the result means evaluating your options to decide which one most closely meets the constraints and results you need to achieve. Depending on the nature of your problem, use either the simple pros and cons approach or the more objective multi-criteria decision analysis approach where you have multiple non-uniform criteria that need to be considered. Be on the lookout for irreversible solutions when you make your evaluation. These types of solutions may be appropriate but may also take away valuable optionality in future. And for high stakes problems, before you lock in your final decision, take a step back and let distance allow any suppressed insights, untested assumptions or emotions flow to the surface that otherwise have been hidden. This helps offset the influence of our judgement junkie, subconscious biases and limiting beliefs.

Pros and cons approach

The pros and cons method is one of the simplest ways to evaluate your options when solving a problem. By listing the advantages (pros) and disadvantages (cons) of each solution option, you can quickly compare options and get a clearer sense of which might offer the most benefits or minimise downsides. It works well when you need a fast decision on a low-stakes problem. For example, if you're choosing between two office locations, you might list the pros, like cost or proximity to clients, against cons, like rent or available space. This can help you get to a decision without overcomplicating things.

That said, the pros and cons method has its limits, especially when things get more complex. It doesn't let you weigh how important each factor is. A minor pro might seem just as important as a major con. Take choosing a new software system, for instance. If one of the cons is months of downtime during installation, that could easily outweigh several smaller pros like saving money on licensing, but a basic pros and cons list won't capture that distinction.

Another issue is that it doesn't really help with uncovering hidden biases. If you're already leaning towards one option, you might end up stacking the list with more pros to justify it. Plus, it doesn't account for how factors might influence each other. Sometimes one pro can directly create a con, or vice versa.

The pros and cons method is great for quick, simple decisions, but if you're dealing with a complex problem, where weighing factors or avoiding biases is key, you'll want a more structured approach, like multi-criteria decision analysis.

Multi-criteria decision analysis approach

Multi-criteria decision analysis (MCDA) is a practical way to evaluate complex options by weighing up multiple factors. Instead of focusing on just one element, like cost or speed, MCDA helps you look at the bigger picture, considering all the aspects that matter.

Once your options have been developed, you start the MCDA by identifying the criteria that will guide your decision. Write down the most important features of solving the problem that need to be considered. The result you need to achieve and the constraints identified earlier are a good starting point. As you've now better understood the problem, other important factors in choosing between options will likely pop up. These will all form decision-making criteria you will apply to evaluate your options.

Your list of criteria should number between five and eight of the most important factors to help guide your decision. Too many criteria causes decision paralysis. Below are some examples to consider:

- **Ease**: how easy is the solution to develop and implement?
- **Cost**: what costs will be involved in planning, procuring and implementing the solution?
- **Durability**: how durable do you need the solution to be? Should it last for a few weeks, or much longer?

- **Speed**: how fast do you need the solution to be implemented and the results achieved?
- **Value**: what specific financial or other value measures do you need to achieve and how close must the solution be to achieving it?
- **Risk**: how much uncertainty and unknown aspects of developing and implementing the solution are there?
- **Impact**: how disruptive to other parts of the business will developing and implementing the solution be?
- **Irreversibility**: will choosing one option make subsequent choices unviable?
- **Scalability**: how important is it that the solution be available for a wider purpose that just solving the immediate problem?
- **Compliance**: how important is complying with laws, regulations or conventions?

Next you assign a weighting or level of importance to each criterion, so you're clear on what matters most. You can use percentages or raw numbers as weighting. I typically use percentages as it's easier to see how close a solution is to perfectly solving a problem by comparing the result to 100%.

Consider assigning 'Hell yes!' or 'Hell no!' criteria. By this I mean, regardless of whether other criteria are met, if this one criterion is not met, then the option is not viable. For example, if it is cost-sensitive, then set a 'Hell no!' criterion at the level of cost that is acceptable. If the results of the evaluation show cost is above or likely to be above this criterion, the option is a 'Hell no!'.

Now you are ready to conduct your evaluation. To do this, assign a score for each criterion depending on how closely the option meets the criteria. These scores can be numbers or simple rankings, like high, medium, or low. If using numbers, you multiply those scores by the weights you assigned earlier to get a final, weighted score for each option. Add up the scores for each option, and the one with the highest total usually stands out as the best choice. Check that your 'Hell yes!' or 'Hell no!' criteria are met for the option you choose.

MCDA is all about making sure you don't get stuck focusing too much on one thing and miss the bigger picture. It gives you a clear, structured way to evaluate each option fairly, based on what's most important to your decision and achieving the results you need.

Beware irreversible options

When evaluating options, think about whether any are irreversible. Where if you choose them, there would be significant consequences that cannot be reversed.

While swimming at a surf beach on the Gold Coast in Queensland in my late twenties, I was pounded by a large wave that hit the left side of my head like a brick. Water surged into my left ear with such force it burst my eardrum. The pain was seriously unpleasant. A trip to see a doctor afterwards revealed something more sinister, however.

After having a look at my eardrum, the doctor told me that he saw something that looked like a tumour. It wasn't an ordinary burst eardrum. A week later I went to see a specialist who told me I had a cholesteatoma: a tumour-like growth of skin cells behind my eardrum that was very close to the sensitive small bones in my middle ear that give you balance and allow you to hear. He told me it had to be removed, or it would lead to permanent hearing loss, vertigo and ultimately death if it ate further into my skull.

This problem needed a solution. The specialist I saw told me he would drill a hole into my ear to remove the growth and after that I wouldn't be able to swim again and would have to be careful in the shower. I didn't like that option, so I went to see another specialist. He told me he would perform the same procedure.

A third specialist had a different approach. He said he could remove the cholesteatoma, repair my eardrum with microsurgery, and replace the bone that had been eaten away by the growth with a combination of drilled bone from the back of my skull and what he referred to as 'bone glue'. He told me I would need two surgeries, a year apart, and it would be very painful. I asked him whether this form of surgery could be performed if I had had the surgery proposed by the other specialists. He told he wouldn't be able to because it would create too much damage for him to repair.

Looking at my options, I decided to go with the painful reconstructive surgeries. My reasoning was that if it didn't work, I could always fall back on the other approach. But I couldn't do it the other way around. I had the two surgeries and luckily have been fine since.

Some options are irreversible. Where the problem is significant and multiple options are being considered, expose the options that are irreversible and have those as flags to consider as you decide what to do. An irreversible option may be the most appropriate, but not always.

Create distance before deciding

It's all too tempting to arrive at a choice on how to solve a challenging problem and be persuaded by a flood of emotion to just take action. To move from the pain of uncertainty to the comfort of doing. Most of us feel more comfortable doing than being in what can feel like an endless contemplation cycle until the right solution is found to a problem.

Creating distance before making a big decision allows time to detach from the immediate emotional intensity, and step back and evaluate the situation with greater clarity. In high-stakes situations, emotions like fear or excitement can narrow your focus, causing key details and critical assumptions to be overlooked. Taking a pause before deciding helps calm these emotions, enabling a more rational and thoughtful approach and gives you a chance to uncover details previously not seen or thought about. It's the 'let's sleep on it' wisdom that gets handed down from generation to generation.

Distance also enhances perspective. When immersed in a problem, it's easy to get tunnel vision, focusing too much on short-term fixes or over value easy to adopt solutions. Stepping back creates space to analyse the broader context and consider alternative strategies that may have been missed. It helps make decisions align not just with immediate needs but also with long-term objectives.

In 2009, Captain Chesley Sullenberger faced a significant and immediate problem. Both engines of his Airbus A320 airplane failed shortly after take-off from LaGuardia Airport (New York) enroute to Charlotte Douglas International Airport (North Carolina). Sullenberger faced an overwhelming and immediate crisis. Instead of panicking or rushing into a decision, he created mental distance in the seconds he had. He methodically analysed his options, returning to the airport, landing on a highway, or ditching in the Hudson River. By distancing himself emotionally and focusing on the facts, risks and benefits of each, Sullenberger chose the river, ultimately saving all 155 passengers on board.

Reflecting on the incident, Sullenberger later said, "In a crisis, you must slow down. You must be deliberate. You can't allow yourself to be paralysed by fear."[33] His ability to mentally distance himself from the emotional intensity of the situation allowed him to make the right choices to the problem he had. He didn't have long to create the distance he needed to disconnect his emotions, but by consciously choosing to do so he was able to think clearly.

In the early 2000's the long-term viability of Amazon's business model was being heavily scrutinised post the dot com bubble bursting. CEO Jeff Bezos faced considerable pressure to cut back on investments in long-term projects like Amazon Web Services (AWS) and focus solely on the core retail business. Instead of making a decision to appease critics and shareholders, Bezos took a step back to evaluate the bigger picture.

By distancing himself from the immediate pressures, Bezos considered how AWS could position Amazon for long-term success. He doubled down on the initiative, committing resources to what would eventually become one of the company's most profitable business ventures. Bezos's ability to create distance from short-term challenges allowed him to make a decision that aligned with Amazon's long-term strategy, transforming the company into the $2 trillion business it is today.

Bezos has said, "The thing about innovating is you have to be both stubborn and flexible, more or less simultaneously. If you're not stubborn, you'll give up on experiments too soon. And if you're not flexible, you'll pound your head against the wall, and you won't see a different solution to a problem you're trying to solve." His ability to step back and view problems from a wider perspective gave him the clarity needed to strike the right balance between immediate action and achieving best long-term outcomes.

ALISON'S PROBLEM

Problem statement
We are currently being paid 30 days after invoice date, which is too slow. We need to receive at least $2,000,000 of customer payments within 15 days of invoice date starting in September and have this continue for at least the next two years to improve our cash flow.

Further investigation
Alison called her team together to refine their ideas into options that could be considered and tested.

Sandra started the conversation, confirming there were at least 30 customer contracts that would have to be renegotiated and changed to meet the target of $2,000,000 early customer payments each month. All except three customers were in Sydney. The other three were based in Singapore and represented 30% of the value of monthly invoice payments.

Customer discounts for early payment had never been offered before and, based on what Sandra and Jimmy said, it was not a standard practice in the industry. Introducing a new idea like this may be successful, they thought, but it would depend on the customer choosing to opt in. The only way to know for sure was to test the idea with customers.

Sally confirmed that altering customer contracts would take at least 40 days and was not guaranteed to be 100% successful, and likely 50% successful at best. She believed in some cases they would need to provide an incentive to reach agreement with their customers to pay earlier.

Each customer contract had a two-year term and was renegotiated three months before expiry. Sally suggested they could include the 15-day payment terms in each new contract and renewal so they would all be updated within the next two years.

OPTIONS TO BE EVALUATED

Customer early payment incentive
Offer an incentive of up to 5% discount to customers if they pay in 15 days instead of 30 days.

Renegotiate customer contracts
Open negotiations with customers to revise contracts to have payment terms of 15 days instead of 30 days.

Secure debtor financing

Secure a debtor financing facility from a finance company where they pay within 15 days of invoices provided to them.

CRITERIA TO EVALUATE OPTIONS
Alison made a list of the criteria they would use to evaluate the three options, asking for input from the team. They developed the following list:

Value: $2,000,000 needs to be paid within 15 days of invoicing each month.

Certainty: There needs to be 100% certainty of at least $2,000,000 of customer invoices being paid within 15 days every month.

Cost: Pay a discount or fee of up to 5% of invoice value to bring the cash flow forward to 15 days payment.

Banking: No increase to the limits or modification of existing financial loans and facilities.

Speed: The new arrangement needs to start within 90 days.
Durability: The solution needs to work for at least the next two years.
Disruption: Limited impact to customers in the short term.
Each criterion was given a percentage, adding up to 100%, to compare each option consistently.

Criteria

Value: 20%* 'Hell yes!' criteria
Certainty: 20%* 'Hell yes!' criteria
Speed: 20%
Cost: 10%
Durability: 10%
Disruption: 10%
Banking: 10%
Total: 100%

To make the evaluation simple and consistent, a score out of 10 was used to indicate how closely the option being considered would meet the criteria.

Applying these criteria, Alison and the team evaluated the three options as follows:

	%	Customer Incentive		New Contracts		Debtor Financing	
		Score	Result	Score	Result	Score	Result
Value*	20%	8	16%	6	12%	10	20%
Certainty*	20%	6	16%	4	8%	10	20%
Speed	20%	6	12%	6	12%	10	20%
Cost	10%	9	9%	8	8%	7	7%
Durability	10%	6	6%	10	10%	8	8%
Disruption	10%	7	7%	5	5%	7	7%
Banking	10%	10	10%	10	10%	10	10%
Total	**100%**		**83%**		**65%**		**92%**

*'Hell yes!' criteria

Alison and her team concluded that the debtor financing option would be the one to present to her boss as the best solution. It met both 'Hell yes!' criteria of having high certainty the $2,000,000 would be paid each month and that it could be implemented within the 90-day window. The downside is the cost, which could be 6% of invoice value which is outside of the 5% constraint given to the team, but only marginally.

Alison asked the team to reflect on the preferred option they had chosen and come back at the same time tomorrow with their final thoughts. She said, "it looks like this solution is a clear winner, but I want you to challenge the assumptions we have about it, think of anything we may have missed and come back tomorrow prepared to ask the questions of us that others would naturally have."

Alison and the team came back the following day for a final conversation about the recommended approach.

Alison asked if anyone had any final concerns or ideas that needed to be discussed. Jim said, "we haven't considered the longer-term view enough I think." "Within two years each contract will be renewed, and each contract renewal can take us a step closer to having these new payment terms embedded within our business," he explained.

As a result of this conversation, the team decided to recommend each new contract be required to include 15-day payment terms as part of the negotiation, so that within two years they could retire the debtor finance facility if necessary and save the finance fee.

Alison presented the proposed solution to her boss, Mike, who liked the proposed solution. Alison then sent an email to Jessie, the CEO, with the proposal. She was nervous, but hopeful it would be received well.

Jessie called Alison later that day and said, "Great work, the proposed solution seems the right fit for what we need. I look forward to seeing how you plan to make this happen." Elated by the feedback, Alison scheduled another workshop with her team to work through the details of how to make her solution work.

Plan and implement the solution

After you've chosen the best option to solve your problem and achieve the result you need, it's time to do what people enjoy most—taking action! It's tempting to rush off and implement the solution you've developed. Where you have people, resources, timing and other factors to consider, it's smart to spend some time working through *how* to best take action before you act.

Your plan of action should address these five considerations.

1. Focus

Start with what people want to know first: why is this a problem, why does it matter, and what do you know about how its caused? Paint a picture of what the future will be like once you have solved the problem. Your focus is a summary of the *reason* you have a problem, *result* that you wish to achieve by overcoming it, and the essence of your proposed solution. If necessary, confirm what will *not* be included in the solution, to avoid any doubt or confusion.

2. Actions

Create steps to show to see how the problem will be solved. Describe the change that your solution will deliver and why this will benefit the business and those who are affected. This is where you describe your chosen *response* to solve your problem.

Usually between four and eight steps are what people can understand. There may be lots of smaller actions below each step, but having a series of steps people can follow and understand will bring confidence in your solution.

If there were other options that were considered and rejected, consider describing what those choices were and why this is the best solution. Your work maximising the result and considering the constraints will help you describe why other options were not as strong as the option you chose.

3. Risks to avoid

Implementing change necessarily involves managing some uncertainties; things that might happen and that would be undesirable if they did. They're called risks. And it's normal to have them when you solve problems.

No plans are foolproof and when met with reality, adjustments will always need to be made. Understanding where the main areas of uncertainty are and how these might impact on delivering your solution is very important. Where you have risks that could have a financial impact on how you solve your problem, allocate an amount of cost to each of these risks as contingency for your budget. Usually, the higher the likelihood of the risk, the higher the amount of contingency needed.

4. Resources

Solving problems often requires resources such as time, money, people, assets and locations. Take some time to consider what resources you will need to help you solve your problems and, where you need to, secure access them.

If you need to prepare a budget to keep track of your costs and secure approvals from your organisation, make sure you budget with sufficient contingency to allow for unforeseen events that may arise.

Contingency is a 'buffer' amount added on top of a cost budget to provide additional resources in case they are needed. The more risk and uncertainty in the work you will do, the more contingency you will need. Between 10% and 30% of costs is a typical contingency amount.

5. Result

Describe what measures will you use to evaluate when and how the problem has been solved. Be specific and consider whether data is available to measure your success before you lock in the measures you will use. Not all data is available and reliable.

For example, if your problem is related to customer complaints about long wait times in a call centre, one measure of success could be reducing the average wait time to a specific target, such as from 10 minutes to three minutes. To evaluate this, you might use call-tracking software that logs and averages call wait times. However, if this data is unreliable or inconsistently tracked, the measure won't accurately reflect whether the problem is being solved.

Similarly, if your problem is to improve employee satisfaction, you might measure success through regular employee engagement surveys. But before committing to this measure, you'd need to ensure that the survey questions are well designed to capture the true sentiments of employees, and that the data is gathered consistently over time. If the surveys aren't conducted regularly or if participation is low, the data might not be reliable enough to evaluate the success of your solution.

If the problem involves, say, reducing production waste in a factory, you could measure success by tracking the reduction in raw material use and comparing it to output levels. This would require accurate data on inventory and production outputs, and if that data isn't easily available, you might need to find an alternative metric or a way to collect more reliable data before finalising the measure.

Red team testing

The concept of red team testing originated in the US military. It was devised to simulate adversary actions and test the robustness of a plan and identify and adjust for weaknesses in advance. Its focus is to challenge and improve a plan by looking at it from an opposing or critical perspective. It involves setting up a group (the 'red team') to poke holes in your plan, find flaws, and expose weaknesses you might not have seen. The point is to stress-test your plan by simulating real-world challenges before they hit.

This approach is crucial for solving highly complex problems, where uncertainty is high and surprises are inevitable. For example, if you're planning a new product launch, a red team could help you anticipate market backlash, competitor responses or operational breakdowns you didn't think about.

The key is to give the red team free rein to stress-test and find problems without sugar-coating anything. Once they've done that, you can take their feedback and refine your plan, strengthening it where it was vulnerable. Red team testing makes your solutions tougher and more resilient by forcing you to face the hard truths before reality does. It's about prepping yourself to handle challenges with fewer surprises, giving your plan a much better chance of succeeding.

Final thoughts

You should now have a viable solution and plan of action to deliver it. A great outcome! No two problems are alike. Adapt the methods in this book to suit the problem you need to solve. Remember, the essence of a problem-solving strategy is to:

1. Understand the **Reason** you have a problem.
2. Choose the **Result** you need to achieve.
3. Develop the **Response** that best delivers the result you need.

ALISON'S PROBLEM

With the assistance of her team, Alison developed the following plan of action to implement her proposed solution to the problem of wanting customer invoices to be paid faster.

PLAN OF ACTION

Focus

We are currently being paid 30 days after invoice date, which is too slow. We need to receive at least $200,000 of customer payments within 15 days of invoice date starting in September and have this continue for at least the next two years to improve our cash flow.

Our solution is to secure a new debtor finance facility to meet the September deadline. We will also progressively negotiate new customer payment terms of net 15 days as customer contacts fall due over the next two years to reduce reliance on the debtor finance arrangement.

Actions

There are four steps to solving this problem:

1. Secure debtor financing

To achieve a fast and competitive result, we will run an expression of interest from three finance companies over two weeks to find and secure the most suitable and competitive debtor finance facility.

Our goal is to have invoice payments made to us within 15 days of invoice date, but ideally much sooner than that at a cost of below 5% of invoice value. We may need to stretch to 6% based on initial feedback, but are hopeful we can negotiate a deal closer to 5%. We will negotiate a two-year arrangement that can be scaled back if necessary over that time.

2. Contact customers and secure approvals

We anticipate at least 30 customers will need to participate in the new debtor finance arrangements to meet our goal. A plan for which customers to contact and who will make the contact is being developed by Sandra in Sales. Any legal documentation required will be managed by Sally in legal.

3. Amend our systems and processes

We will develop new processes and amend our systems for invoices to customers who are part of the debtor finance arrangement. We may include wording on the invoice that it is subject to debtor financing arrangement. We will prepare communications for all affected parts of the business to make sure changes are understood and made in time. Final decisions on changes in processes will be coordinated between Sally, Sarah and Jimmy in operations.

4. Amend payment terms on new renewals

All of our customer contacts will renew over the next two years. A policy will be developed to require customer renewals to include 15-day payment terms. Sarah and Sally will coordinate this with the Sales and Legal teams. We are hopeful that within the next two years the majority of customer payment terms will be 15 days. At that point we will consider whether the debtor finance facility needs to be retained or retired. Phil from finance will alert the finance team to put this facility on review annually for the next two years.

Risks to avoid

Our biggest risk is time. We have 20 days of contingency to make sure we hit our deadline. We will have daily stand-up meetings for the first two weeks to establish momentum and confirm actions are on track and make sure we stay on top of any actions that slip behind.

Resources needed

We will need the support from Legal, Finance, Sales, Customer billing and Treasury to run the debtor finance tender. Phil from Finance will lead the tender process. The work will be part-time, two hours a day for the next six weeks, until we complete the tender and understand the changes needed to systems.

We may need a small budget of $5,000 for programming support to change our invoices for the customers that become part of the debtor financing arrangement. We won't know if we need this until we complete the tender and understand how the processes work with the financial institution we select.

Result

We will track the value of invoices paid within 15 days from 1 October, a month after we are expecting the first wave of debtor financing payments to be made. Each month after that we will separately report the value and days of invoice payments to show how we are progressing and attribute them to either new contract terms or debtor financing, to show which solution is delivering the results.

Next steps

Alison wrote an email to Jessie to explain her plan of action to solve the customer payment problem. Jessie called her and said, "Great job, you have my approval to take the actions you suggest and receive the support and resources you need. I look forward to seeing the results."

CHAPTER 15

Develop the Response (Part 2)

- Depending on the nature of your problem, use either the simple pros and cons approach or the more objective multi-criteria decision analysis approach to evaluate options and maximise your result.
- Use 'Hell yes!' or 'Hell no!' criteria to filter out marginal options.
- Be on the lookout for thinking traps that can skew your decision-making. These include the bandwagon effect, the certainty effect, confirmation bias, loss aversion, the framing effect and the sunk cost fallacy.
- Before you decide, consider carefully whether any options are irreversible.
- Develop a plan that has a clear focus, actions, resources, risks to avoid and measures for success.
- Before you execute your plan, consider requesting a 'red team' to critically evaluate your plan and help uncover challenges that can be solved before you take action.

3R Problem Solving Strategy Guide

	① Understand the Reason	② Choose the Result
Steps		
Description	Understand the reason to solve the problem by describing the situation clearly, confirming it matters and finding its causes.	Choose the specific results you need to achieve and identify the constraints that must be considered to reach them.
Actions	• Describe the situation. • Determine whether it matters. • Find the causes.	• Decide what results you need. • List the constraints.
Outcomes	• Initial problem definition. • Decision to solve the problem or not.	• Final problem definition. • Decision to proceed to find solutions to the problem.
Insights	• The problem you define is the problem you solve. Make it the most important issue. • A problem is when we need to do or have something but don't, or when we are doing or have something we don't need. • A problem matters if it has significance to value, time, status and wellbeing. • To get to the root cause of problems use the 5-Why method and Hypothesis-based testing approaches.	• Define the results you need in terms that can be easily measured. • Pitch results at the right level. Never aim too low. • Align stakeholders to the results you need to clear a path for cooperation and support. • Describe the results you need using language that provides the widest range of potential solutions to consider. • Mindfully select input, process and output constraints to optimise creativity, motivation and productivity.

③ Develop the Response

Description	Develop a response to the problem by creating a solution that maximises the results needed within given constraints and create a plan of action to achieve it.
Actions	• Recruit the right support. • List causes as opportunities. • Identify options. • Maximise the result. • Create a plan of action
Outcomes	• Committed and capable team. • Options to evaluate. • Recommended solution. • Plan of action to solve the problem and deliver results.
Insights	• Recruit people with the right capability, influence, capacity and desire to solve the problem. • Switch problem cause for questions to stimulate creativity. • Explore changing what you do or changing what you have to develop options. • Generate ideas by using inversion, solo brainstorming, hero switching, starbursting, outsider peer perspectives and PMI techniques. • Group and evaluate options using an objective evaluation technique to maximise the result. • Use "Hell Yes" criteria to filter out marginal options. • If close enough isn't good enough, rework solution elements or push against constraints to find the right solution. • Create a plan of action that has a clear focus, actions to take, resources needed, risks to avoid and measures of success.

CHAPTER 16

Find help that propels you forward

"You can't put a price on the experience of having great people around you."
Shane Warne

I used to be terrible at asking for help. I happily gave advice or support to anyone who asked, but for a very long time I was hesitant about putting my hand up and getting the help I needed most. Asking for help for me felt like I was offering myself up for a ritual flogging or swallowing medicine that tasted worse than rotting fish given to me by a well-meaning doctor. Sometimes it felt like both. And I just didn't like it.

But not asking for help when you need it just makes the job of solving problems much harder than it needs to be. And worse, it can keep you stuck for far too long. What helped me open the door to asking for help was when I realised it was as much about me learning to prepare myself to ask for help as it was about when, how and who I asked for help. Both are important to make sure you get the help you need when you need it.

How to be more open to support

Nobody wants to feel less than how they hope others perceive them. Or put another way, nobody likes to feel dumb in front of others, particularly our colleagues and bosses. Most of us don't like feeling vulnerable at all. But not wanting to feel vulnerable can lead to being reluctant to ask for help and advice when we need it.

Feeling vulnerable can lead us to feel like impostors, where we think we are incompetent and hope like crazy that others don't find out. So we avoid asking for help all costs. Because if we do ask for help, our mind makes us believe the people we ask will start to think we are in fact incompetent, and our façade of brilliance will be broken. And not long after that we believe we will be shown the exit door and our careers, lives and reputation will be in tatters.

Not asking for help when you need it just makes the job of solving your problems much harder

Feeling like an impostor is in the same family of feelings as embarrassment and shame. These can be super-toxic emotions if we let them take hold of us. It's understandable, then, that if we connect asking for help to feeling like an impostor, we will do whatever we can to avoid asking for help. It becomes a self-imposed prison.

Here's a little secret: we all feel like impostors when we start something new that we haven't done before. No one skips this step on their path to developing new skills. It's how we know we're in the right spot and we're learning. And it's okay.

I felt this way for many years, even when I was a partner at EY. It wasn't until a senior partner said to me, "We aren't meant to know everything, you know, Spike." He called me Spike on account of my short spikey haircut at the time.

"It's why we are in a partnership", he said. "Our clients expect us to bring the best of our collective thinking and experience to them, so it shows greater strength and intelligence asking for help than trying to be a hero on your own."

That made me sit back and think. I thought I was being stoic and valuing my ability to do everything myself when really, I was limiting my potential by not asking for help when I could have from those around me.

I then learned how to drop my reluctance to ask for help. I wish I had done it sooner. Some days I still struggle asking for help, but I now know I can reframe my thoughts when I fall into this trap to help me get the help and advice I need.

Getting comfortable asking for help means shifting these two limiting beliefs to more positive ones.

Limiting belief: I am the results of my work

At work, we are rewarded and punished in many respects for our output and our contribution. It is normal to be assessed on completing tasks to an expected quality and within a certain timeframe, hitting targets for sales, production or profitability. But measurement can reinforce some people's thought that we are what we do, because it's what is focused on the most.

Achieving what we are required to do in our roles at work is important. But it's not *who* we are. It's just *what we choose to do*.

To become more open to asking for help, we need to separate ourselves from our work. If we allow our identity to be dominated by our status and the output of our tasks, then we allow ourselves to become attached to what people think of us. That leads to believing that if our work is criticised, we are being criticised as individuals. And thinking this way makes it very hard, if not impossible, to ask for help. It makes us react defensively when we receive advice, even if the advice has value and is given with respect and care.

Shifting the basis of your identity from what you do to who you are can be a significant process to undertake. What started this process for me was looking at my life as a whole; seeing my values, beliefs, passion projects, relationships and pathway to growth alongside what I chose to do to serve society and earn money as a more holistic picture of me as a human.

Each part had its pluses and minuses. The biggest shift for me came in re-examining my values and choosing to pursue a life that consciously lived those values, and not just living to work. The shift in thinking I made was going from 'I am what I achieve at work' to 'I am a balance of how I think, feel and behave at home and at work'. Thinking of myself this way meant I could be on a learning path at work. If I'm criticised, it's only one part of me, not all of me, and that was okay.

Limiting belief: Asking for help is a weakness and character flaw that will reflect badly on me

In some workplaces, asking for help and feedback is compulsory and seen as a sign of strength. Pixar established a 'Braintrust' to provide directors with feedback on films that were in development, because in every film, at some point, no matter how experienced the director is, they get lost in creating the film and have trouble seeing what's not working or is causing a problem. It's a normal phase of movie production. And asking for a Braintrust session was viewed as a sign of strength, not weakness.[34]

For the feedback to be received well by the director, they had to feel confident that it was normal and expected if they were stuck working something out. And everyone goes through that. The Braintrust process was normalised for every film. It was expected and important and, as a result, no one took the feedback personally. Asking for help was expected and shown to deliver the best results.

How to find the right help

It's normal to feel like you don't know who to ask for help when you first need it. I suspect not many people have a network with every possible expert available to them. But you will always be able to find a person to talk to who may know someone, who may know someone who can help you. We are all no more than six degrees of separation from one another.

Simon Dobbin is a production designer and art director who worked in Hollywood for over 20 years. He helped make dozens of movies, commercials and music videos in that time. He once worked on a comedy film with a scene that needed an Olympic-sized pool to be filled with yellow water. The pool had to be yellow to give the impression someone had urinated in it and it had all turned yellow.

Two weeks before the scene was to be shot, Simon set his mind to finding a solution to the problem of turning the pool yellow. The solution needed to be fast, cost very little, and have no risk of unintentional damage or consequences – such as having to rebuild or repair the pool at significant cost or turning all the actors who jumped into the pool yellow for a few weeks. None of these would be good outcomes.

His first idea was to use yellow food dye. He poured some into a glass and hey presto—yellow water. So he set off to a local food supply store, bought a large quantity of yellow food dye and poured it into the 'test pool', which was in the backyard of the film producer's home. It didn't work. The food dye turned clear within minutes of being poured into the pool. Simon thought to himself, "Maybe there wasn't enough food dye". He went back to the food supply store and bought triple the quantity and poured that into the pool. Same result. Clear water. He was stumped.

Other options he considered were draining the pool and painting the tiles with removable yellow silicone paint. The pool was huge, it was a daunting and time-consuming task. After the scene was shot, he would have to drain the pool again and remove the yellow paint. Simon discussed this idea with the local pool managers, and they told him if he did that, there was a risk the pool would 'float up' and crack because it needed the weight of the water to keep the ground from rising up beneath it. Not surprisingly, this option was ruled out.

He concluded he had to work out how to get yellow food dye to work in the pool. He thought there must be a reason the yellow food dye wasn't working in the pool but did in a glass of water. The only difference he could think of between the glass of water and the water in the pool was the presence of chlorine and other chemicals. Maybe this was the part of the problem that needed to be solved, he thought.

He now needed help. He had done all he could to understand the problem, and he had tried to solve it himself. He now needed advice from someone who knew more about how chlorine, water and food dye worked together than he did.

Simon had previously worked with science and product advisers from 3M, the industrial products company famous for making adhesive tape and those yellow Post-it Notes. They are very clever at understanding the chemistry of things. He gave Rick, his contact at 3M, a call, and described the problem, what he had done to understand and solve it and where he thought the path to a solution might lie—learning more about how food dye, chorine and water interacted.

Rick made some calls to colleagues at 3M. He eventually found the world's leading expert on chlorine —an 85-year-old lady named Elsa who lived in Hamburg in northern Germany. She didn't speak English, but through an interpreter she said she could help solve Simon's problem.

Rick called Simon the next day and told him the good news. Simon was both ecstatic and relieved. On the call, Elsa told them, through an interpreter, that chlorine acts to neutralise the chemical properties of food dye. The solution to turning the pool yellow was to stop the chlorine acting in this way. And to do that, all Simon needed was apple juice. "Apple juice neutralises the effects of chlorine", she said. Elsa just needed to know the volume of water in the pool, the chlorine level, the presence of any other chemicals and the water's pH level. Once she had these details she said she could calculate the quantity of apple juice and yellow food dye needed.

Simon provided the required details to Elsa, and she told him the precise amounts of juice and dye to use. It was hundreds of litres of apple juice and food dye. And it worked. Simon now had a yellow pool. And a very happy director.

There was just one remaining question: how to turn the pool back to clear water. Elsa said, "Just pour chlorine back in". Shortly after finishing filming the pool scene, Simon poured chlorine back into the pool and within seconds it looked like it had never been yellow at all.

Your network of friends, family, colleagues and social media connections could all provide a stepping stone to get you the help you need to solve challenging problems you are working on. Even if you don't know the exact specialisation or experience you need, describing the problem in enough detail will make it easy for anyone to help you.

Judge advice you receive carefully

A former neighbour of mine is an emergency physician. He's one of those doctors who jumps into the helicopter first when there's been an accident in a remote location, and someone needs medical assistance.

I asked my neighbour one day, "How do you know what action to take when you only have a few minutes to diagnose the situation and save someone's life?" He told me that it all comes down to pattern recognition.

You see, our bodies are all pretty much the same, except for the reproductive organs. There are quirks for sure, but we all have a heart, need blood and have lungs to capture oxygen that we need to survive. He told me the context of all the problems he had to deal with was always broadly similar. So, the advice he would give to help save someone's life can be taken as being very solid. That's because he's seen similar problems many, many times and our bodies are all pretty much the same.

But business isn't always like this. In fact, the context of problems in a workplace shifts constantly. The experience of someone who may have seen a similar type of problem years before may be directionally helpful, but not contextually useful now.

It's the same with our intuition. Our subconscious sees patterns and tells us, "Hey I think I've seen this before, it doesn't feel right". It's a good warning sign, but it may not have all the facts and be as useful as we think. Intuitions are only trustworthy when the judgements they are based on are built up with experience in familiar and predictable environments. In other words, the experience and advice of others needs to be weighed against the environment of the problem you are facing. If the environment is very similar, then the advice or experience has more relevance than if not.

CHAPTER 16

Find help that propels you forward

- Seeking support to solve problems is a sign of strength, not weakness.
- Feeling vulnerable when solving challenging problems is normal. It's a sign you are shifting into a learning zone.
- Judge advice you receive based on the relevance and currency to your specific problem.

CHAPTER 17

Choose the opposite way

"You cannot look at a problem the same way as everyone else and expect to find a new solution."
Edward de Bono

Colin Grant was 25 years old and was searching for a way to create a better life for his young family. He'd done well as a franchise owner of a Mexican fast-food restaurant in his hometown of Canberra, Australia's capital city, and thought to himself, "What if I can do this again, start up or run another business?"

Searching through classified advertisements in the local paper, Colin found an opportunity to purchase a struggling microbrewery, The Canberra Beer Company. Confidence started 'brewing' inside him. He decided to go for it and become a beer baron.

Colin met with the owners of the microbrewery and struck a deal to buy the assets and the business on deferred settlement terms, which would give him the time he thought he needed to fix the business and generate enough profit to pay the vendors. The business had a great product, he thought, but revenue had been declining to the point of no longer covering operating costs. He thought the business had a simple problem to solve—they weren't selling enough beer.

Colin made a list of all the pubs within 20 kilometres of his brewery. He jumped into his car with two fridges filled with ice and samples of his beer and set off for the first pub on the list. He arrived there soon after it opened at 10 a.m. and asked for the bar manager. He had his pitch ready to go. Jim, the bar manager, greeted him with a firm handshake, and they sat down at a table a few metres from the main bar. Colin took out the pitch deck he had prepared and started talking to Jim about how his beer tasted great, how it was brewed locally and how amazing it would be to supply it to this pub. Jim listened patiently to Colin as he made his pitch.

When he'd finished, Jim said, "Colin, we have 10 taps in this pub as you can see, serving 10 different beers. Eight of those taps are owned by the major brewer that installed them for us. We have to buy beer from them for those eight taps. I only have two taps I can use to buy from other brewers. And every week I have at least five breweries pitching to supply beer to me."

"Ah", Colin sighed. "So, all I can offer you is a spot on my waiting list to call when it's your turn. We only allow two weeks of supply from every brewer. That way our regular patrons always have something new to choose from," Jim explained.

Colin left the meeting feeling dejected. That was just the first pub. Surely, it's not all the same as this, he thought to himself. Within six weeks of taking the keys to his new brewing business, which he had no prior experience working in, Colin learned two important things about it that reshaped his understanding of his problem.

1. Most pubs to which he could supply beer were already locked into contracts with major brewers. In these contracts, the suppliers provided the taps, fridges and other equipment for 'free' in return for committing to only selling their beer on the majority of taps they provided.
   This meant most pubs had only two or three taps available for other breweries to supply, which significantly increased competition for microbreweries like Colin's.
2. Bar managers preferred to rotate the beers they purchased for the 'uncontracted' taps roughly every month, so their customers always had something new and interesting to try. This was causing roughly 80% of customers to stop buying

beer from him within a month of signing a contract. Which meant virtually all sales needed to be replaced every month to just maintain existing revenue, which was a huge challenge to keep up with.

It was a problem that Colin had to solve quickly. He worked out he had about two months to turn sales around to avoid a cash flow crunch that he couldn't recover from. At the same time, his then wife was pregnant with their first child. They were living in a converted shed in the backyard of a pleasant but eccentric elderly man's house. He needed to solve the problem not just to save the business, but also to provide a real home for his young family.

Colin worked out he needed to sell a minimum of five kegs of beer per customer per month and retain each customer for at least six months to survive. And he needed to do this without spending very much money on marketing or new product development.

Using a two metre by three metre whiteboard he had installed in a corner of the brewery, Colin wrote down the questions he thought he needed to answer to solve his problem:

1. How do we stand out from other brewers to make more sales?
2. When we land a new customer, how do we stay there for six months?
3. How do we do it without spending money?
4. How do we do this in less than two months?

This formed the checklist he used to evaluate his ideas. The first idea he came up with was to start selling his beer direct to consumers and not to pubs. "I had seen another brewer in the UK struggle with the same challenge and their answer was simple. If we can't get any bars to sell our beer, we'll buy our own bars and then sell our beer through a chain of our own pubs and bars", he told me.

Colin looked at starting his own bar but found local government restrictions prevented on-site direct-to-consumer sales in their suburb. They didn't have enough money to relocate the brewery.

He investigated buying pop-up and mobile bars as well as making and selling boutique 'kegerators' (a little fridge with a keg inside and beer tap on top) direct to consumers. He ruled these out after discovering they were too expensive to set up and pre-purchase.

He also looked at other distribution channels, including selling to liquor retailers. But it would take at least five weeks to develop and have ready a packaging solution to meet retailer requirements, which was too long to make this a viable solution.

Colin had to find another way—and fast.

One night, after all his staff had left work for the day, he wrote down all his ideas on his whitebeard on the brewery floor. He figured if he wrote them all down and stood back and stared at them, he might see the path to a solution.

Colin was worried, nervous about the future, but optimistic about finding a path out of this mess and giving his family the home he wanted for them.

To keep himself thinking positively, he kept asking himself, what if we win? He didn't want the negative thoughts and worries about failing and letting his family and friends down to cloud his creativity to come up with solutions.

"My stomach turned in knots when I looked at the numbers, but I genuinely believed we could turn it all around", he said to me. Colin knew enough about himself to know that his best thinking came when he was moving, not sitting in a chair. Early one morning before the sun had risen he took himself for a long walk, letting his mind wander, searching for alternative ways of looking at the problem. The cool Canberra air wrapped around his body like blanket pulled from the chiller in his brewery.

He wrestled with his thoughts, telling himself to start from a place of positivity to let the ideas flow, to allow new connections to form. Colin started thinking about whether seeing things from the opposite perspective, to look at the problem from the other side, would generate new ideas.

He thought to himself, every craft brewer thinks they have the best beer. People selling beer walk into the same bars with the same pitch, something like, "My beer's the best, please buy my beer, your customers will love it".

He had a flash of inspiration. Rather than sell pubs our beer and tell them why it is good for their customers, why not sell them their beer? he thought. Instead of saying "Buy my beer" we could say, "How would you like to make your own beer'?" he thought.

His mind started racing. He could feel the beginning of a solution falling into place. Pubs could come up with their own beer name and flavour profile, guided by our brewmaster. We could invite the bar staff to the brewery to participate in making their beer and really let them take ownership over it, he thought. Once the bar staff had made the first batch, his team could take over and make any additional batches for them.

After selling their beer to them, when pub customers walk into a bar and ask the bar staff, "What is this new beer, is it any good?" passion would pour out as they spoke in detail about the flavour profile and the ingredients and the entire brewing process because they created the beer. It was their beer.

Then, rather than giving up the tap to the next craft brewer each month, anytime the bar wanted to try a new beer they would come back to the brewery and simply repeat the process and make a new variety.

Colin found a way to get 'unstuck' in his thinking and free his mind to look at how he could solve the problem from the opposite perspective. This change in thinking was a masterstroke.

His new solution was:
- differentiated
- addressed churn
- didn't cost money to implement
- could be implemented immediately

Colin pitched his idea to two bar managers the next day. Instead of pushing the benefits of his product, Colin simply said, "How would you like to buy your own beer from me?" It was the opposite of what they were used to hearing. Bar managers were intrigued by it. After considering it for a few minutes, they loved the idea and wanted to move forward with a purchase.

Within six months, Colin and his team had increased sales by 300% and achieved an 80% retention rate for new customers. He had found a solution to his problem of not selling enough beer by looking at the problem from the opposite perspective. And this turned out to be the right way to go.

Inverted thinking

What Colin used to create this solution was *inverted thinking*, where you look at a problem from the opposite perspective to generate new ideas. It's a strategy that's been widely used by philosophers, mathematicians, musicians, artists and entrepreneurs for generations to find solutions to challenging problems.

Ask, "What if the opposite were true? What if I focused on a different side of this situation?" Instead of asking how to do something, ask how to *not* do it.

Consider this situation: a herd of sheep is slowly making its way down a narrow country road flanked by steep banks. In a rush, a driver approaches from behind and urges the shepherd to move the sheep aside to allow the car to pass. The shepherd declines, explaining that he can't ensure all the sheep will stay clear of the vehicle in such a tight space. What would you do to solve this problem?

Using inverted thinking, the shepherd reversed the situation by asking the car to stop. He then calmly turned the flock around and guided them back past the waiting vehicle.

Richie Blackmore, guitarist in the 1970s rock band Deep Purple, used inversion to come up with the riff for the song Smoke on the Water, considered to be one of the most iconic in rock history. Richie was fan of Beethoven. One evening he was playing Beethoven's Symphony No. 5 and wondered what it would sound like if he played the notes backwards. That thought was the genesis for two musical bars that make up the iconic riff for the song *Smoke on the Water*.

SpaceX used inversion to revolutionise spaceflight with reusable rockets. Traditionally, rockets were single use, resulting in immense costs as each launch required building an entirely new vehicle. Rockets like the Atlas V or Delta IV are expendable, and cost anywhere between $100 million and $400 million per launch, depending on the vehicle and mission. Instead of accepting this as a given, SpaceX inverted the problem: what if rockets could be reused, like airplanes, to dramatically reduce costs?

Looking at a problem from the opposite perspective will generate new ideas.

This shift in perspective led SpaceX to focus on designing rockets capable of surviving re-entry, landing safely, and being refurbished for subsequent missions. The Falcon 9, for instance, features a first stage equipped with landing legs and precise thrusters, allowing it to return to a landing site or drone ship. The estimated costs are about $62 million per launch when factoring in the cost of the rocket and the reuse process, a significant advantage over competitors. SpaceX claims that the reusability of the first stage alone can save approximately 30-50% of the total cost of a launch. If they can reuse a Falcon 9 first stage up to 10 times, the cost per launch could decrease substantially due to amortisation of the initial cost of building the rocket.

In the late 1970s, pop artist Andy Warhol was searching for a way to boost sales and wondered how he could use his bestselling works to inspire related works that could sell just as well. Experimenting in his studio, Warhol took his best-known artworks, including his coloured prints of Marylyn Monroe, created more than 10 years earlier, and swapped the light colours for dark ones and switched shadows for vibrant colours. It was an experiment that gave birth to his *Reversals* collection—reinterpretations that were the inverse of the originals. The Marylin collection of *Reversals* sold for more than double the price of his originals.[35]

In 2019 Scooter Braun purchased the original recordings of Taylor Swift's first six albums, and she lost control over how her music was distributed and marketed.[36] This meant that anybody who wanted to licence any of Swift's old songs for a movie or TV show would have to get Braun's permission and pay him a fee. Taylor had previously wanted control of her recordings and had lobbied to buy them back from Big Machine Records, which she has been signed to. She was very upset at not being given the chance to own the rights to her own music.

Taylor's problem was: "Braun has control over the original recordings to six of my albums, and I want to own them". Instead of raising hundreds of millions of dollars to buy the original recordings from Braun, Taylor decided to create her own recordings, *Taylor's Versions*, of the original albums.

Instead of *buying* what she didn't have, she chose to *create* what she didn't have. She would then have control over any new recordings and not have to fight Braun for them or pay hundreds of millions. Taylor has since recorded three new versions of her previously recorded albums.

Inverted thinking can also be used to identify future pitfalls that might be overlooked when focusing only on success. This helps in proactively managing risks and planning around obstacles that could derail progress. For example, instead of asking, "How can we improve customer satisfaction?" ask, "How can we make our customers extremely dissatisfied?"

Consider the following questions to help you use the power of inversion to solve problems you are working on.
- Can you **switch** the elements of the problem for their opposite? Change light for dark, backwards for forwards, them for you, it for any, up for down, positive for negative energy, manual for digital or firm for flexible.
- Can you find a way to **see** the problem from the opposite perspective? For example, customer perspective for supplier perspective, using pictures and not words, attributes for feelings, start for end.
- Can you **experience** the problem in the opposite way? How it would not happen versus how it would happen, what the result would do vs what the journey would do.
- Can you **include people** who are opposite to those who are working on the problem, to generate new ideas? People with opposite skills or people who are not currently working on the problem at all.
- Can you **flip how time is used** when solving the problem? Change slow for fast, bursts of time for steady time usage, or how each element of the problem uses time.
- Can you **change the location** of the problem to be opposite of what you have? Centralised vs decentralised, on the ground vs above ground, or moving vs stationary.
- Can you **exclude something** rather than try to fix it to solve the bigger problem?

CHAPTER 17

Choose the opposite way

- Innovative solutions to problems can often be found by looking at the situation from the opposite perspective. It's called inverted thinking.
- Inversion has been used for generations by artists, musicians, mathematicians, entrepreneurs and business leaders to find creative solutions to challenging problems.
- Switch elements of the problem or solution, such as time, people, location, inclusions and the framing of the problem to see if it sparks ideas otherwise hidden from view.

4
A Problem Hunter's Capabilities

OVERVIEW

Capabilities are combinations of learned skills, cognitive abilities and mindset that enable us to perform tasks effectively, efficiently and repeatedly. It's how we get things done. In this fourth and final section, my aim is to provide you with an understanding of four essential problem-solving capabilities and the skills that support them to help you identify your unique strengths and opportunities for growth. It can also serve to help identify how teams can work together better to solve problems.

Knowing a method to solve a problem is useful only where it's matched with having the capabilities and skills to put that method into practice. The four essential problem-solving capabilities are pathfinding, connecting, producing, and tasking. These capabilities balance the forces of ambiguity, certainty, leading and doing; forces that are integral to solving any complex or challenging problem.

For each capability I've defined six key skills from my experience, and supported by research, that contribute the most to exceptional problem-solving capabilities. Chapters 18 to 21 describe these skills and the beliefs and the strategies that will help you master them.

Learning to learn faster provides a significant advantage to accelerate your problem-solving skills. Your rate of learning and the retention of new knowledge combine to lift not only your skills but your overall intelligence. In Chapter 22 'Learn to Learn Faster', I provide you with strategies to increase your rate of learning and retention of new knowledge so you can progress faster.

Finally, a note of caution and optimism on multitasking. It's a common productivity strategy to try and solve multiple problems at once, but it can fail badly where you need to perform deep work on one of them. Science has proven we can't focus deeply on more than one task at a time. Multitasking can be useful, but only where appropriate safeguards are in place and for the right type of problems.

Four essential problem-solving capabilities

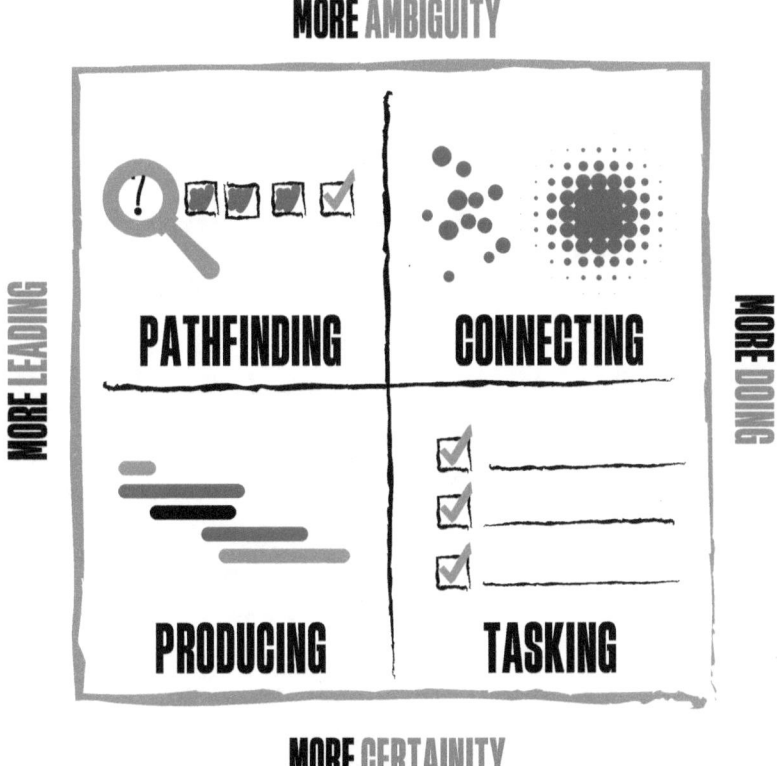

Pathfinding: Providing direction and certainty when facing the unknown.
Connecting: Developing and joining ideas, people, know-how and capabilities to create new discoveries. It's the essence of creativity.
Producing: Sourcing and coordinating resources, fostering collaboration, and delegating and controlling tasks that combine to drive progress.
Tasking: Mastering and completing discrete activities that underpin progress.

CHAPTER 18

Pathfinding

"The person that clears the path, controls its direction,"
Ryan Holiday.

Pathfinding is where you create certainty and direction when surrounded by the unknown. When first faced with a problem, pathfinding provides the clarity and calm needed to determine what steps to take to start making progress. To assess whether there is a problem and, if so, what the path is to solve it and to be in command of your emotions and reactions when walking through the anguish of uncertainty.

When someone is lost, they often ask, "Can you show me the way?" Solving problems can make people feel lost if they don't know what to do next or what they should be aiming for. Pathfinding provides a direction and the steps to take when a way doesn't exist.

In 1914 explorer Ernest Shackleton led an Antarctic expedition aboard the *Endurance*. The ship became stuck in the pack ice of the Weddell Sea in January 1915, and by October of that year it was crushed by the ice, forcing the crew to abandon ship. After drifting on the ice for months, Shackleton and his crew took to lifeboats in April 1916. They reached Elephant Island in May 1916, but the island was too remote for any chance of being found.

Shackleton and five of his men then embarked on an 800-mile (1,300 km) journey across the rough South Atlantic in a small lifeboat to South Georgia Island to seek help. After arriving on the island, they crossed its rugged, mountainous interior to reach a whaling station on the northern side. After several failed attempts to reach Elephant Island due to ice conditions, Shackleton finally rescued the remaining crew on 30 August 1916, almost 22 months after the *Endurance* had become trapped in the ice.[37]

Despite the hardships, he found a path to rescue all 28 men from the *Endurance* expedition. Shackleton famously said, "Difficulties are just things to overcome, after all".[38] This story of courage and finding a path through what would have been harrowing conditions to save his crew is an extreme example of pathfinding but illustrates the point that finding a direction and continuing to move forward despite the obstacles put in front of you is an essential problem-solving capability.

> **Pathfinding is providing direction and certainty when facing the unknown.**

Pathfinding is where you clear a path for others to follow, set the result and goals needed, and lead people towards achieving them. It's where you provide clear communication and reassurance that inspires and maintains momentum. It's where you influence others of the merits of solving a problem and help them find the courage to solve it.

Anita Roddick founded The Body Shop in 1976, creating a retail environment that prioritised environmental sustainability and social responsibility long before these concepts became mainstream. Roddick's vision was to use business as a force for good, promoting fair trade and cruelty-free products. Roddick said, "If you think you're too small to be effective, you've never been in bed with a mosquito". She believed in the power of individuals and businesses, no matter their size, to make a significant impact on challenging problems.

Yvon Chouinard, the founder of outdoor apparel and equipment company Patagonia, established the company in 1973 and was an early pioneer in using business to address environmental issues, emphasising sustainable practices throughout Patagonia's operations. He cleared a path for others to follow. He said, "The business is not the main thing, it's the engine for change". Ultimately, pathfinding is creating the environment for change to flourish.

Get comfortable with discomfort

You don't need to be a visionary entrepreneur or explorer to become skilled at pathfinding. But you do need to learn how to tolerate the discomfort of not knowing.

But how do some people seem to be more comfortable sitting in the fog of unknowing than others? They appear calm and clearheaded when others around them are panicking because there is a problem and they don't (yet) know what to do about it. The key to answering this lies in how our minds treat two conflicting but simultaneous truths. The first is that when we are faced with a problem of significance, not knowing what to do about it causes fear.

Fear of the unknown is one of our most common and paralysing emotions. For most people, walking into a dark room and hearing a sudden creak makes your heart start racing. Your mind swirls with all the horrible things that could be lurking in the shadows. Our survival instinct kicks in and our imagination runs wild. We seem to intentionally traumatise ourselves as a way of being on high alert and ready to respond to extreme danger.

The second truth is that challenging situations provide a great opportunity to create significant value and learn new skills. It's knowing that what appears threatening at first is often not as bad as it seems, and that with the right focus, a solution can be found.

Pathfinding skills

Pathfinding focuses on creating a vision for the future that overcomes the limitations of the present and influencing others to follow in pursuit of that vision.

Visioning

Visioning is seeing beyond immediate challenges, defining goals and objectives that set the focus and direction for others. It includes defining what is important, ignoring or deprioritising what is not, and aligning resources and energy with these intentions.

Three key visioning skills to master:

- **Strategic thinking:** Seeing the wider context of a problem and understanding the long-term impact. In problem-solving, it means understanding how a single challenging situation fits into the bigger picture, allowing you to focus on addressing root causes rather than just surface-level symptoms. It requires analysing the wider context, such as the environment, stakeholders and future consequences, to predict how different solutions may affect long-term outcomes.

- **Goal-setting:** Setting long-term goals and breaking them down into smaller clear objectives. Longer-term goals shape the results and expectations that need to be achieved. Breaking the ultimate result down into smaller objectives helps to move you closer to a final solution, making complex problems feel more approachable. Each smaller objective acts as a milestone, allowing you to measure progress and build confidence as you move forward.

- **Deciding:** Prioritising what is important and making informed and timely decisions that maintain momentum and focus to achieve results. Deciding is determining what matters most and taking action that builds momentum towards achieving the results you need. Prioritising the right decisions ensures you stay on track, avoid unnecessary detours and keeps the problem-solving process moving forward.

Influencing

Influencing is guiding others' thinking, decisions, and actions without needing to exert direct authority, being agile and adaptive to change.

In a work environment, solving problems that matter will most often require working with people you have no direct authority over. You need influencing skills to break through competing priorities and merge interests with action. It helps align diverse viewpoints and gain buy-in to support a point of view or direction. Influencing skills build trust and consensus, which is crucial when solving complex issues. Done well, influencing fosters a cooperative environment where ideas and solutions are more readily accepted, magnifying problem-solving efforts.

Three key influencing skills to master:

- **Communicating:** Clearly articulating thoughts and requirements in a way that inspires and motivates others to follow. Communication lays the groundwork for collaboration and understanding among team members. When you articulate your thoughts and requirements clearly, you help everyone grasp the problem and the shared outcomes needed, minimising the risk of misinterpretation or confusion. It creates a sense of shared purpose and commitment that drives collective effort towards a successful solution.

- **Negotiating:** Engaging in discussions with others to reach mutually beneficial agreements and resolving conflicts. It's not just presenting your viewpoint, but actively listening to others, understanding their perspective, and finding common ground. It requires steely determination and balancing empathy and compassion. Solving problems requires resolving conflicts, aligning diverse interests and creating deliverable solutions.

- **Switching:** Pivoting and adjusting strategies and actions in response to changing conditions and new information. Switching involves being open to new information that highlights unexpected challenges and having capacity to adapt and change. It's being willing to pivot and adjust your strategies to respond effectively to changing circumstances, ensuring that you don't become rigid or stuck in one approach. Flexibility is crucial for maintaining progress. It allows you to explore alternative solutions and capitalise on new opportunities, ultimately leading to more innovative and effective solutions.

Beliefs that support developing pathfinding skills

Here's a list of the limiting beliefs I've found get in the way of mastering pathfinding skills and suggested alternative, empowering beliefs to counteract them.

Limiting beliefs	Empowering beliefs
I believe I need to act quickly to solve all problems to be seen as strong and capable.	I should take swift action to understand a problem first, then act with haste only if needed to solve it quickly.
I believe I can't solve hard problems that I haven't solved before, so I shouldn't try.	I can find a way to create solutions to any problem by learning a method and finding the right support.
I believe if I try and solve hard problems and fail, it will be bad for my career and reputation.	Showing courage, diligence and having humility to learn and adapt are attributes that will enhance my career, not hold it back.
I believe only the most clever and experienced people can develop a path to solve hard problems.	With practice and growth, anyone can learn how to develop a path to solving hard problems.
I believe if I put my hand up to solve a hard problem, I will put too much pressure on myself and my mental health will suffer.	If I work on progressively harder problems, like working out in a gym, I will become more capable.

Strategies to develop your pathfinding skills

Study philosophy
The works of classic Greek stoic philosophers Seneca, Epictetus and Marcus Aurelius provide a wide range of considerations for how to prioritise what is important and how to manage your emotions to make sensible strategic choices.

Read decision-making and negotiation texts
Making choices, particularly under stress, is a great skill to learn. Ask your colleagues, friends or a mentor what has helped them become more confident in making decisions. There are many good decision-making and negotiation books to choose from. Study and practice their techniques.

Practice staying calm when uncertain
Uncertainty creates fear because it's viewed by the mind as a threat, unless we reframe and tame it. Here are three ways to train yourself to stay calm during uncertainty:

1. Reframe uncertainty as opportunity
Instead of viewing uncertainty as a threat, shift your mindset to see it as a space for potential growth and opportunity. Focusing on positive rather than negative aspects of a situation creates calm and reduces anxiety. Consciously bring your mind back to the positive if you find it dwelling on the negative for too long. Practice using this perspective when you're not facing uncertainty so that it's familiar when you do.

2. Learn to trust your judgement
It can be tempting to respond to uncertainty by turning to existing road maps. While they are helpful and provide a path for your mind to follow when uncertain, over-relying on methods creates dependence that can derail your sense of control when they don't fit what you need. Learn to trust your own judgement, to create room to break the

rules and turn processes into tools that can work better and harder for you. The more you learn to trust your judgement, the more in control you feel.

3. Focus on what you can control

Feeling in control brings a sense of calm. To tap into this, identify the parts of the situation you can actually influence and focus your energy there. By homing in on what you can control, you shift your mindset to actions and thoughts you can impact. Taking action is reassuring, especially when you're dealing with uncertainty.

Find a mentor

Even the most successful CEOs have a mentor to help develop their perspectives. Pathfinding is a skill of perspective, and the growth of this skill is greatly accelerated by having someone more experienced to learn from, where you can be vulnerable about not knowing something and feel safe to learn.

Ask questions of others

Ask these questions of people who have experience you want to learn from about how they developed a path to solve a problem:

1. What was your thought process when you first encountered the problem and what helped you respond the way you did?
2. What was your initial perspective on the problem and how did that influence your approach and how you engaged and directed others?
3. In hindsight, what would you have done differently to understand and respond to the problem and why?

CHAPTER 18

Pathfinding

- Pathfinding requires being comfortable with ambiguity and leading others. It involves determining whether a problem is worth solving and setting a clear goal that provides direction throughout the problem-solving process.
- Strategic thinking, goal-setting, deciding, communicating, negotiating and switching are key pathfinding skills to develop.
- Fear of the unknown and loss of control is natural, but learning to tolerate discomfort allows you to stay focused and create the space needed to find the right path to solve a problem.
- To develop your pathfinding skills, read the works of the classic Greek philosophers and decision-making texts, find an experienced mentor to guide you, practice strategies to stay calm when uncertain, or seek out the experience of others to learn from.

CHAPTER 19

Connecting

"Creativity is just connecting things. When you ask creative people how they did something, they feel a little guilty because they didn't really do it, they just saw something. It seemed obvious to them after a while."
Steve Jobs

When I was five years old, I loved books with pictures you could create by connecting numbered dots. What started as a random page of dots with numbers would reveal a hidden picture when you joined them in the right sequence. I felt excited by the process of joining things together and discovering what picture it would reveal.

Problems require you to find relevant ideas, people, know-how and capabilities (dots) and connect them to help understand the situation better and create solutions. Sometimes the dots aren't yet visible, so you need to go hunting for them. At other times, what you need can be found right in front of you. The skill of finding dots and joining them is how you connect your problem to a solution.

The connecting capability is about bringing together ideas, capabilities, people and resources to spark new discoveries and creative solutions. It involves blending diverse knowledge, insights and experiences to create something novel. Those who excel at connecting see relationships and opportunities where others see separation and silos. They are adept at joining different elements to develop a more comprehensive understanding of the problem and generate solutions that might not have emerged otherwise. This capability is the essence of creativity and innovation, because it combines elements that may seem unrelated at first glance but, when put together, unlock new possibilities. Everyone has the ability to see and join things together. All it takes is to free your mind and let possibilities flow through you.

British billionaire Richard Branson has created dozens of successful businesses using his connecting skills. In an interview, Richard told the story of how he came to start Virgin Airlines. The founder of Virgin Records was 28 years old at the time and was trying to board an American Airlines flight in Puerto Rico to get to the British Virgin Islands to see his future wife, Joan Templeman.

He explained, "The captain comes on the speaker and says, 'Sorry, the plane has not got enough passengers. You will all have to come back in the morning'."

> **The connecting capability is about bringing together ideas, capabilities, people, and resources to spark new discoveries and creative solutions. It's the essence of creativity.**

Instead of accepting disappointment at this flight not being available, Richard's connecting skills went into action. He said, "I go to the back of the airport and pull out my credit card as ask, 'do you have any planes I can rent?' And they did. So, I chartered one. I borrowed a blackboard, and I thought 'What am I going to call my airline? Virgin Airlines sounds good.'"

"I wrote Virgin Airlines, one way ticket $39 [on the blackboard] and I went around to all the people that were bumped [off the flight] and filled my first plane. We arrived in the BVI [British Virgin Islands], happy Joan, happy me. The next day I thought 'screw that'. I asked for the telephone number of Boeing. I got through to Boeing and said, 'Hello, my name is Richard Branson. Do you have any second-hand 747s for sale?'"[39]

We may not all have Branson's financial resources or bravado, but we can learn the principles he uses to create innovative solutions to challenging problems.

Branson found a solution to his problem by connecting two new ideas:

1. I can't use your plane, so can I get my own?

He needed to develop a new solution, so he looked at the problem of not having a plane from the opposite perspective to find an opportunity.

His original solution that failed was travelling on *someone else's* plane. He then wondered, "What if I travelled on *my own* plane?" This gave him an idea to pursue, a new 'dot' to see if it could be joined to find a solution.

Given time was a major constraint, Richard wondered how he could quickly get his hands on his own plane. Borrowing one was the best way to acquire something he needed to have within the timeframe. This was possible by chartering a plane, so he had the beginnings of a workable solution. He found a dot to connect a new solution to. But he needed one more 'dot' to make it viable.

2. It costs a lot to charter a plane, can I get others to help pay?

Richard started selling tickets to offset the cost of chartering the plane. He advertised directly to other passengers bumped off the flight, which enabled him to fill the seats on his plane. He had a solution that was now viable.

What Richard instinctively did was break the problem down into its cause and looked for options to overcome it by changing what he had from travelling in someone else's plane to finding and using his own. He found alternative 'dots' to connect together to form a new solution.

Connecting is joining ideas and capabilities together that create new solutions.

Connecting people to problems

Connecting is also how you join people with different experience and expertise that combine to create new ideas and solutions. You've probably experienced this at school and in the workplace. Some people are fabulous at connecting what one person is seeking with another that may have an answer.

Mike Cannon-Brookes understood the value of collaboration, both internally and externally. Atlassian, the Australian software company he co-founded with Scott Farquhar in 2002, fostered partnerships with other tech companies and educational institutions, believing that collaboration is essential for innovation. "Innovation is about connecting ideas, and bringing different people together", he believes. Atlassian now has a market capitalisation of over $50 billion.

People who connect problems with people are vital to problem-solving.

Connecting skills

Connecting consists of experimenting and exploring.

Experimenting

Experimenting is using ideas, parts, processes, capabilities and technology in unfamiliar or novel ways to create something new. Conducting experiments, engaging in free-flowing, spontaneous play to spark new ideas to pursue. Experimenting is the purposeful invention or discovery of something new.

Three key experimenting skills to master:

- **Analysing**: breaking down complex ideas and subjects to understand their components, patterns and relationships. Analysing allows you to dissect a problem into first principles and manageable parts, making it easier to identify factors and relationships that can be used to create solutions. Examining a problem at first principles and the constraints that exist help uncover underlying patterns and insights that may not be immediately apparent. It leads to a deeper understanding of the problem, enabling you to target effort and resources towards finding creative solutions.

- **Testing**: combining disparate ideas, information and other inputs to form new concepts or approaches and confirming viability.
Testing involves blending various ideas and data to assess its practicality and suitability. It allows you to explore different combinations of insights and approaches, providing a safe environment for experimentation without the fear of failure. Ideas need to meet with reality to create viable solutions.

- **Resilience**: persisting in the face of challenges and setbacks while experimenting with new connections.
Challenges and setbacks provide the feedback needed to create the right solution to a problem. Resilience provides the energy and focus to keep pushing forward despite obstacles arising and failures occurring. It involves adapting positively in the face of challenges, maintaining emotional stability, and continuing to make progress. By remaining resilient, you can experiment with new ideas and connections, continuously refining your approach until you discover a solution that effectively addresses the problem and drives progress.

Exploring

Exploring is searching for and finding something you need but don't have. It's where you develop specifications for something you believe will help understand a problem or solve it, and discover where it exists. It's where you pursue and assimilate ideas and the work of other people to help find new insights. It's like hunting for and finding buried treasure.

Three key exploring skills to master:

- **Imagining**: generating a wide range of ideas and concepts to reveal new or hidden connections.
  It involves thinking and exploration beyond conventional boundaries or what's immediately obvious. Feeling the freedom of possibility and expression of what could be without constraints. Imagining is the fuel that powers innovative solutions.

- **Collaborating**: networking and facilitating working with others to blend different skills, knowledge, and ideas that generate new insights.
  Collaboration extends the capacity for connecting problems with solutions by simultaneously accessing the collective wisdom, talents and experience of multiple people. Diversity of viewpoints spark new connections, saves time learning, and fosters a sense of shared ownership and commitment among team members, increasing the likelihood of successful solutions.

- **Curiosity**: asking questions, exploring new ideas and being eager to discover how things do and don't work.
  It's developing a desire to learn, explore and understand new information, experiences, materials or concepts. Curiosity propels you to ask questions, seek out knowledge and investigate the unknown, feeding a mindset of inquiry and exploration. Curiosity leads to critical thinking, allowing you to challenge assumptions, uncover new insights, and connect what was previously unknown to create greater understanding.

Beliefs that support developing connecting skills

Here's a list of limiting beliefs I've found gets in the way of mastering connecting skills and suggested alternative empowering beliefs to counteract them.

Limiting beliefs	Empowering beliefs
I'm not good at coming up with new ideas because I'm not creative.	I believe creativity is a learned skill like all others, and what I choose to focus on, I can develop.
I won't be able to solve the problem because I don't have enough expertise or experience in the problem I need to solve.	I believe not having a lot of experience with a problem is an advantage as it lets me see things from a new perspective.
If I try but fail, I will be ridiculed, and my career will be affected.	I believe hard problems will always need trial and error to solve them. I can do difficult things.
I'm not patient or confident enough to keep experimenting and trying to find an answer to help me solve the problem I'm working on.	I believe that there are always answers to problems if I persist and ask for help when I need it.
Feeling out of control and not knowing how to solve a problem is the most painful thing to experience and I will hate it if I linger there too long.	I can control my emotions and reactions and, with practice, can learn to tolerate this feeling like any other.

Strategies to develop your connecting skills

Be more divergent

There are two types of thinking processes when it comes to finding new and creative ideas to help solve problems:

1. **Convergent thinking:** where you judge ideas, criticise them, refine them, combine them and improve them, all of which happen consciously.
2. **Divergent thinking:** where you imagine new ideas; original ones that are different from what has come before, but which may be rough to start with, and which often happens subconsciously.

Convergent thinking, which is the easier of the two types, is most commonly taught in schools. Divergent thinking, however, is where the unique and most creative ideas emerge, but it requires a bit more effort. This is mainly because it involves managing the uncertainty of not knowing the answer and the time it takes to develop ideas while remaining in that state of uncertainty.

Practice using these questions to develop your divergent thinking and notice how you feel the longer it takes to arrive at an answer. The longer you can tolerate the discomfort of not knowing, the greater your divergent thinking capability will become. You can't use up your creativity. The more you use it, the more you have available to use.

Divergent thinking questions
What if...?
How can we...?
Why is [this] happening in this way?
What would happen if...?
What can make [this] faster, cheaper, lighter etc?
Who can help shed a new light on [this]?

Let walking and sleeping power your connections

If an idea or solution isn't coming to you as you need it to, take a walk or sleep on it. Our brains are designed to think better as we move. Walking helps improve creative thinking by an average of 60%.[40] Steve Jobs was famous for conducting meetings while walking. Even after going for a walk and sitting down, creative thinking is still higher than without going for a walk.

Our brains are wired to help us solve problems as we sleep.[41] While our conscious mind is asleep, our subconscious does its job of finding connections. Our subconscious mind is much better at finding connections between disparate memories and ideas than our conscious mind is. Give your subconscious the task of finding inspiration to the challenge you are working on just as you turn out the lights before falling asleep. Your mind will go to work creating connections to inspire you in the morning. Usually, within the first two hours of waking, an image or thought will flash in my mind that takes me a step closer to finding the answer I need or directing me where to look.

Use it so you don't lose it

As we age, we focus more on doing and leave less time for creating. It's a natural atrophying phenomenon. But in the same way that muscle mass starts to deteriorate from the age of forty unless you get back into the gym and do weight-bearing exercise, your creativity will become harder to access unless you start using it regularly.

By age thirty-one we can lose up to 98% of our creative problem-solving skills.[42] But there is a way to reawaken it. While you're at work, look for opportunities to practice your connecting skills by diving into the following types of activities:

- **Brainstorm a problem:** This forces your mind to seek connections, strengthening the brain's neuroplasticity capacity.
- **Conduct tests and trial new ideas and tools:** This leads to new discoveries and awakens curiosity.
- **Develop new business proposals:** This connects the brain's creativity and practicality together.
- **Develop new processes:** This connects analysis, collaborating and imagining skills.
- **Test and develop new services or products**: This develops imagining, testing and analysing skills.

Get out more

We tend to drift towards being creatures of habit. Our minds go to sleep easily when we do the same thing over and over in the same environment. Author and expert on creativity Jonah Lehrer said, "Distance and difference are the secret tonic of creativity".[43]

We need to regularly make our brain uncomfortable by spending time in unfamiliar places and thinking in ways we normally wouldn't.

Pablo Picasso's view was, "The chief enemy of creativity is good taste". Make it a priority to spend time each week in places you've never been, do things you haven't done before and challenge your closely held beliefs. Even better, get out for a few weeks and immerse yourself in a new culture, language and climate. It's like an ice bath for the mind!

Your capacity for creativity is influenced directly by having more diverse experiences you can connect to form new ideas. Gathering a wider range of experiences enables you to more easily connect ideas and create something new. People with limited or narrow experiences often lack enough varied insights to make new connections, leading to straightforward solutions that may not fully capture the complexity of the problem. "The broader one's understanding of the human experience, the better design we will have", Steve Jobs believed.

Create space for your brain to be creative

When you need a boost to your creative capacity, disconnect from the barrage of information we get each day. Go someplace remote and away from other stimulation. We are flooded with information every day. The average amount of information a person absorbs daily is estimated to be around 34 gigabytes and roughly 100,000 words. This includes information from social media, emails, conversations, entertainment and other forms of digital and non-digital content. We can't consciously process all this information, so most of it is stored in our subconscious mind. Creativity works best with a quiet and focused mind where the subconscious is free of other distractions.

The more distractions and content we need to process, the less able we are to let our minds do the work we want them to. Authors famously hide themselves away to focus their creative skills. Roald Dahl, Mark Twain and George Bernard Shaw all used remote getaways to write some of their most famous works. Artists similarly use their studios to block out external stimulation, and bands use recording studios to do the same.

Distraction is often a result of unmet emotional needs and external triggers, rather than a lack of willpower, according to Nir Eyal, author of *Indistractable: How to Control Your Attention and Choose Your Life*. To become 'indistractable', he argues, you first need to understand your internal triggers, and address them directly to remove the temptation.

Notice when you become distracted from challenging thinking and what your instinct is to soothe yourself from the discomfort. Identify what the trigger is and take action to address the source to avoid further, repeated distractions.

Use anger as motivation for action

Anger is a very helpful emotion for motivating action. What is frustrating, annoying and makes your blood boil can be turned into fuel to take action to find a solution. Follow the path of your frustrations and instead of complaining, challenge yourself to connect potential solutions to the problem.

Use anger to flex your creative muscles rather than letting it go to waste. Even if you don't present your solutions to someone who can authorise your changes, consider it a practice session to build your creative skills, like a basketball player shooting hoops by themselves. No one sees it, but it helps them develop their skills.

Be more vulnerable to find better solutions

Pursuing the unknown can make you feel vulnerable to criticism, failure and shame. University of Houston professor Brené Brown defines vulnerability as: "The emotion that we experience during times of uncertainty, risk, and emotional exposure".[44] She further says, "Vulnerability is not winning or losing; it's having the courage to show up with you can't control the outcome".

Practice allowing yourself to be more vulnerable. Vulnerability as a character trait is not a weakness. In fact, it's a superpower because it opens the door to building greater trust and more authentic communication with others, which makes a significant difference to how new ideas are shared, built on and developed into solutions.

Being vulnerable means being open to being wrong. It's holding the belief that no one is perfect and everyone continues to learn. Where people feel open and free to express their ideas without fear of judgement, it's like swapping a creativity garden hose for a fire hose.

Questions to ask of others

Ask people who have experience from which you want to learn these questions to discover how they developed creative solutions to challenging aspects of a problem:

1. What were the main challenges of [the problem] you had to solve and how were they found?
2. What people and resources were critical to solving [the problem], how did you know they were needed, and where did you find them?
3. In hindsight, what would you have done differently to create the key solutions to [the problem] and why?

CHAPTER 19

Connecting

- Connecting involves combining the untested and unexpected. It's about linking ideas, methods or concepts that seem unrelated or have never been used together.
- Essential connecting skills include analysing, testing, resilience, imagining, collaborating and curiosity. These skills combine to help you bring together different perspectives and resources to solve problems in creative ways.
- Connecting is the heart of creativity. It's about bridging the gap between what you already know and the unknown, allowing you to explore uncharted territory and find new and innovative solutions.

CHAPTER 20

Producing

"Success is not about ideas. It's about making ideas happen."
Scott Belsky

The producer is the driving force behind bringing a film to life, managing the business side of the production while also supporting the creative process. They are ultimately responsible for delivering a completed film that is on time, within budget and ready for audiences. Kathleen Kennedy, producer on several *Star Wars*, *Indiana Jones* and *Jurassic Park* movies says, "A producer is the glue that holds the production together, from the moment the script is green-lit to the final cut being ready. It's their job to make sure everyone else can do their job".

Producing a solution to any problem is just like being the producer of a movie. You need to be able to see what's required, and organise a process to coordinate and control the flow of tasks and activities that combine to progress from discovering or selecting a problem through to it being solved and the results delivered.

The producing capability is about converting plans and ideas into tangible outcomes. Producing is focused on implementation, results and practical execution. In this mode, people take the frameworks and strategies developed through pathfinding and connecting and turn them into reality, ensuring that the problem-solving process leads to tangible results. Their strength lies in efficiency and delivery, taking what's been envisioned and making it happen in a structured and methodical way.

If a team working on a solution were a band, the producer would be the drummer setting the beat to guide the other players to perform their roles and stay in time.

When I was a junior consultant, a partner I worked for gave me his advice on how to become better at coordinating and leading others for the projects I worked on. He said to me "Remember three things: one, be humble, two, be direct and three, be unrelenting." He helped me understand that producing great results means bringing things together and not giving up. I have used that advice throughout my career to help me develop the skills to lead teams to solve challenging problems.

> **Producing is sourcing and coordinating resources, fostering collaboration and delegating and controlling tasks that combine to drive progress.**

People want to work with others who value their contributions, can listen and take on board good news and bad news gracefully, provide direction and challenge where needed. Producing brings all the elements to solving a problem together. Vincent Van Gogh knew this when he said, "Great things are not done by impulse, but by a series of small things brought together".

Progress from what's familiar to what's unfamiliar

Your producing skills will progress through two stages.

1. Producing what's familiar

When you've performed a role and developed expertise in completing the specific tasks required of it, you become confident and capable of directing others to assist you. Where you know what's required to solve familiar problems, you can predict and coordinate others to support you in completing them. It's a typical progression for people to gain more responsibility in their chosen area of expertise.

2. Producing what's unfamiliar

A step up in your producing skills is where you take charge of solving a problem that is outside your area of expertise, as Alison did in the case study in Section 3. This is where you rely on having a method and the skills you can apply to a problem and know it will give you confidence to work through it and solve it.

Producing skills

Producing consists of sourcing and organising the resources needed to solve a problem and controlling them effectively to deliver the result needed.

Organising

Organising skills combine to schedule activities and priorities, arranging people and resources, creating budgets and setting the tasks to complete that will combine to deliver the result you need.

Three key organising skills to master:

- **Scheduling**: Defining tasks and outcomes in advance to ensure what needs to get done, gets done when required.
  Managing time creates confidence and calmness. It provides certainty that others can look to and frame their actions and contributions around. Scheduling involves creating the responsibilities and outcomes needed and aligning them across time to enable a problem to be solved.

- **Delegating**: Assigning tasks and responsibilities to appropriate people based on their capabilities and the contribution needed. Delegating well means sourcing the right support and providing clear instructions. The right support will have capabilities, influence, capacity and desire that align to what you need. Issuing the right instructions involves creating clear expectations of what, when, where and how that you need to happen.

- **Budgeting**: Estimating and allocating financial resources effectively to ensure solutions are created within expectations. Budgeting is a key skill in all organisations and involves estimating labour, materials and other costs essential to investigating, finding a solution and implementing it. It's where you take tasks and responsibilities and create estimates for time and cost along with a contingency for unknowns and risks of estimating error.

Controlling

Controlling skills combine to enable tracking of progress, forecasting what is still required, adapting and shifting where needed and holding people accountable for their contributions and actions.

Three key controlling skills to master:

- **Forecasting**: Recognising potential obstacles and adapting plans and people to manage around them.
  Forecasting is having one eye on what should happen and another on what is likely to happen, and seeing any differences. It's creating an awareness of progress against expectations and determining where what is required may differ in ways that could undermine progress or enhance it. Forecasting provides a view of the future from information that currently exists.

- **Risk management**: Identifying and assessing the scope and impact of uncertainty and taking steps to manage it to within acceptable limits.
  Risk management is about spotting potential problems and deciding what action should be taken to stop them, limit their impact or transfer the potential problem to another party. It's a close cousin of forecasting, but differs in considering the potential impacts across not only time and value, but also on the status and wellbeing of what and who is involved. Where these impacts would become intolerable, actions need to be taken to avoid a problem or its solution from being further affected.

- **Feedback**: Giving and receiving timely and constructive feedback to continue progress and improve outcomes.

  Feedback provides a clear sense of where an individual or team is at, what is working well and what could be improved, and why. The goal is to create awareness, inspire growth and motivation to sustain yourself and a team to complete the work necessary to solve a problem.

Beliefs that support developing producing skills

Here's a list of limiting beliefs I've found get in the way of mastering producing skills, and suggested alternative empowering beliefs to counteract them:

Limiting beliefs	Empowering beliefs
I believe I'm not experienced enough to direct others on what they should be doing to solve the problem.	My knowledge of the problem and appreciation for people and their contributions will be enough to help solve the problem.
I believe asking for help makes me look weak in front of my colleagues.	Asking for help is smart and helps me solve problems faster and more effectively.
I believe I will be taken advantage of by suppliers if I ask for their opinions on how to solve my problem.	By remaining curious and asking why their ideas and solutions are the best fit for my problem, I can determine if it is the right fit for me.
I believe if I trust people too much I will be let down.	If I invite people who have the capability, influence, capacity and desire to help me and treat them with respect and openness, they will find a way to support me in solving my problem.
I believe I can't manage budgets and money because I don't have a finance qualification.	I can learn anything if I choose to focus on it and do the work required. If I don't have the time to learn, I can ask someone to help and teach me.

Strategies to develop your producing skills

Get organised

Producing is developing a mindset that values order and rhythm. Practice breaking large tasks into smaller ones. Use the problem tree method to break your work into problems and solutions to help create a sense of order and connection between what you do and what it means.

Try different planning tools to help you gain expertise in scheduling and forecasting activities and resources. Practice delegating to remove the weight of tasks from you and share them with others.

Be bold

Volunteer at a charity or community organisation, sign up to be part of a community event like a fun run, or ask your manager if you can participate in a project team where you can lead part of the project that has challenging problems to solve. Get out of your comfort zone to stretch your skills and learning.

Do some shadow work

Learning through observation and practice are the fastest ways to develop your skills. If your organisation supports shadow working programs, where you get to experience another part of an organisation to develop your skills, jump at this and ask to work with someone who has a coordination and project management role or a risk management role.

Practice the feedback sandwich

Feedback is best served with a mix of positive and constructive insights. The 'feedback sandwich', which follows the structure of positive message—constructive change message—closing positive message, is a proven method for delivering feedback in a balanced way.

Questions to ask of others

Use these questions to ask people with experience you want to learn from about how they developed their producing capability and skills.

1. What were the main challenges of scheduling and coordinating the work to solve [the problem] and how did you overcome them?
2. How did you keep control of the resources and contributions of those required to support solving [the problem]? What were the main challenges you had to overcome and how did you do it?
3. In hindsight, what would you have done differently to manage the resources and workflow to solve [the problem]?

CHAPTER 20

Producing

- Producing is about execution. It involves identifying necessary resources, coordinating activities, and setting and controlling the processes to move from understanding a problem to implementing a solution.
- Key producing skills include scheduling, delegating, budgeting, forecasting, risk management and giving feedback.
- Developing producing skills progresses through two stages. First, learning to produce what's familiar and second, learning to produce what's unfamiliar.
- To develop your producing skills, practice being more organised, take on managing a new challenge, or shadow a more experienced person with the type of producing skills you want to develop.

CHAPTER 21

Tasking

"Success is the sum of small efforts, repeated day in and day out."
Robert Collier

Tasking is completing the actions that provide the glue that sticks a problem to a solution that creates change. Mastering and completing discrete activities underpins progress. Tasking activities include writing reports, sending emails, gathering data, preparing diagrams, interviewing people, finding suppliers, developing checklists, testing solutions, arranging travel, providing updates and contributing at meetings. It's the actions that are clearly defined and often are repeated frequently. Nonetheless, it is vital they are performed well to make a problem shift to a solution.

These activities form the backbone of effective problem-solving. Thomas Edison understood this well. He once said, "Genius is one percent inspiration and ninety-nine percent perspiration". Edison, through years of experience, knew persistent and diligent execution of routine tasks often leads to groundbreaking innovations.

> **Tasking is mastering and completing discrete activities that underpin progress.**

Steve Jobs recognised that attention to detail when performing tasks leads to extraordinary results. He said, "Be a yardstick of quality. Some people aren't used to an environment where excellence is expected."

We often give the regular tasks we do little thought. They become second nature when practiced enough. The challenge with these types of activities is that our brains can turn off and our minds become reluctant to do them if they don't provide the stimulation we need to stave off boredom. Boredom and complacency are the enemies of tasking. Creating novelty and new experiences for the same activity help turn mundane into memorable. It helps keep the mind adaptive to learning new skills and adjusting to unexpected challenges.

Working from a new location, finding and learning new software to perform the same task, researching and finding new methods to complete the same job, shifting from analogue to digital actions or using video rather than email messages are examples of using novelty to overcome boredom when completing routine tasks.

Repetitive tasks drain our mind of the creative fuel that we need to stay engaged. Use novelty as a strategy to engage your mind to look at common tasks differently. It will provide you with the stimulation to stay focused and adapt to new technologies and methods that improve your productivity and engagement in these activities.

The 15% rule

In performing tasks, we either do what we know how to do, or we have to learn to do something new. The 'sweet spot' for learning and developing your skills is to aim to get 85% of what you do as you learn right. The other 15% of the time you're meant to mess up or get things wrong, because it's these experiences that help reinforce learning.[45] Striving to be perfect is not the best way to learn. You need unexpected errors and mistakes to help confirm what you know and adapt your skills about what you don't. So expect to mess up sometimes, and find a way to learn quickly and share the knowledge you gain with others. See Chapter 22, *Learn to Learn Faster,* for tips on how to speed up your learning and increase retention of what you have learned.

Tasking skills

Tasking consists of performing actions diligently and adapting and developing the skills needed to do them.

Performing

Performing tasks well involves receiving and understanding instructions and requirements, clarifying anything you don't understand, and relating what is required to how it supports the wider goal of what needs to be achieved. It involves being self-motivated to complete what is required and being consistently reliable.

Three key tasking skills to master

- **Clarifying:** Understanding what needs to be achieved and being confident in asking questions to confirm your understanding. Knowing what to do and how to do it is the foundation of tasking. Clarifying what is required of you means being able to repeat back to a person, in your own words, what they expect of you and have them agree. Where there is a difference, seek to understand why and adjust what you need to do. Don't move forward with a task until you have clarified what is expected of you. Important factors are time, outcomes, constraints, resources available or needed, and who you will need to work with.

- **Accountability:** Self-managing work quality before handing it over to others and being accountable for what's required. Accountability is showing care and attention to detail where it's important to the overall result to be achieved. It's taking responsibility for delivering what you've committed to, being proactive in informing others where factors inside and outside your control are impacting what's required of you, and taking steps to work around them. Accountability builds trust, which is essential to solving challenging problems.

- **Consistency:** Being dependable, honest and taking pride in the work completed.
  We all have our bad days, and are forgiven for the occasional slip-up. Consistency means being far more reliable than unreliable.

Consistency builds trust, just as accountability does. It erodes quickly where you become known for being inconsistent.

Adapting

Adapting your skills to complete required tasks means becoming self-aware of your skill gaps and proactively developing them where needed. It means being able to learn from setbacks and being persistent and resilient when progress becomes challenging. It also means finding ways to stay interested in the tasks being performed and avoiding distractions, and seeking to create value beyond simply completing tasks.

Three key adapting skills to master:

- **Focusing:** Maintaining attention on key tasks and minimising distractions to achieve meaningful progress.
  Focusing involves prioritising tasks that align with overall goals and breaking them down into actionable steps. It means minimising distractions and creating the conditions to perform deep work that maintains momentum and progress.

- **Mastering:** Achieving a high level of skill proficiency through focused practice, continuous learning, and the ability to apply skills effectively in various contexts.
  Mastering requires dedication to ongoing development, including seeking feedback and embracing new challenges that stretch your abilities. It includes a commitment to focused practice to develop expertise that increases the value you provide from the tasks and the efficiency with which you perform them.

- **Persistence:** Continuing to work towards competing tasks despite facing challenges or obstacles.
  Persistence is the ability to remain committed to achieving an outcome despite facing obstacles or failures, viewing these challenges as integral to the learning process. It's not giving up when a task requires overcoming barriers within yourself

or externally. It's developing awareness of your abilities and limitations and using them to stay focused and adapt to what's required of you.

Beliefs that support developing tasking skills

Here's a list of limiting beliefs I've found get in the way of mastering tasking skills and suggested alternative empowering beliefs to counteract them.

Limiting beliefs	Empowering beliefs
I believe doing the bare minimum to help solve a problem is a smart and clever use of my time.	Leaning into problems is the best way for me to learn and grow, which will fast track my career.
I believe it is up to others to tell me what they want of me and I will just do it. It's not my job to be proactive. `	If I apply my own thinking to a problem, and show how I can adapt and learn, I will stand out from the crowd and get access to better opportunities.
I believe work is just a way to get money to live.	Work is a pathway to learn and grow my skills and value.
If I can't find the answer or do the task straightaway, I will stop and get someone else to show me or do it for me.	It is my responsibility to try to do what I need to solve a problem, and if I can't, I will learn or ask others to help when appropriate.
If I see a problem outside my responsibility, then it is not my job to point it out or offer solutions.	If I see a problem that could be significant, I will do what I can to understand it and then seek help to draw attention to it and solve it if I can't myself.

Strategies to develop your tasking skills

Develop productivity and distraction-busting hacks

We all have finite time and more to do than we could hope to achieve. Make it your quest to find opportunities to bring smarts to how you use your time. This will give you the space to solve more challenging problems. Discipline is your friend if you want to accelerate getting important work done.

Since the invention of the smartphone, social media apps, video on a phone and instant messaging, our ability to be distracted has become an epidemic.

Strategies I use to bust distraction include *timeboxing*, where you allocate specific time to complete certain tasks and do your best to stick to it, and *my morning muster*, where I use my peak energy, which is in the morning, to focus on the tasks that require deep work.

I focus on this work until noon, with only emergency distractions permitted. I turn off all my notifications and put my phone on silent to let me focus. If I'm in an office, I work separately from others to allow this deep work to happen.

Become a master micro-learner

You don't need to pursue fancy multi-year degrees to learn new skills. There are hundreds of free ways to learn something new. Make a list of new skills you want to learn, either by observing others or keeping up with technology that is changing. If there's a new technology that's available to use, make it your business to try it out and learn it.

Don't wait to be asked: get on it. Ask others what's the most go-to skill they use and how they learned it. Find a faster way to learn it yourself. Take a micro skills course or use an online source to help you get tips on what to do. Make learning as important to your survival as keeping breathing.

Practice focused self-reflection

Take learning into your own hands and develop a practice of daily self-reflection on what you attempted to learn the previous day and what you could improve on.

The discipline of self-reflection might feel a little awkward to start with, but it's how high-performing athletes manage their progress. Being objective and focused on learning is a key that unlocks their potential, so it's taken seriously. If you want to develop yourself faster, treat your progress like that of an athlete.

Questions to ask of others

Use these questions to ask people with experience you want to learn from about how they developed the habits and learning hacks that make them exceptionally productive at completing tasks:

1. What are the habits or routines you've used that helped you develop expertise in this task?
2. How do you approach challenges or obstacles when performing this task, and how has that evolved over time?
3. What was the key turning point in developing your expertise, and how did it help?

CHAPTER 21

Tasking

- Tasking involves completing the repeatable actions that provide the glue that sticks a problem together with a solution to create change.
- Essential tasking skills include clarifying, accountability, consistency, focusing, mastering and persistence.
- Boredom is the enemy of tasking. Use strategies such as changing location and finding a new way to complete a similar task to keep you focused and engaged.
- Making mistakes is part of the learning process. The 15% rule suggests that a 15% error rate is optimal when acquiring new skills. Take calculated risks and don't be hard on yourself for missteps.
- Improve your tasking skills by developing productivity and distraction-busting hacks into your work routines, becoming a master micro-learner and practicing focused self-reflection.

Four Essential Problem-solving skills

Capabilities	❶ **Pathfinding**	❷ **Connecting**
Definition	Leading others and providing direction and certainty when facing the unknown.	Developing and joining ideas, people, knowhow and capabilities to create new discoveries. It's the essence of creativity.
Comfortable with	• Ambiguity • Leading	• Ambiguity • Doing
Focuses on	• Visioning • Influencing	• Experimenting • Discovering
Key Skills	**VISIONING** • Strategic Thinking • Goal Setting • Deciding **INFLUENCING** • Communicating • Negotiating • Switching	**EXPERIMENTING** • Analysing • Testing • Resilience **EXPLORING** • Imagining • Collaborating • Curiosity

	 **Producing**	**Tasking**	Capabilities
Definition	Sourcing and coordinating resources, fostering collaboration and delegating and controlling tasks that combine to drive progress.	Mastering and completing discrete activities that underpin progress.	
Comfortable with	• Certainty • Leading	• Certainty • Doing	
Focuses on	• Organising • Controlling	• Performing • Adapting	
Key Skills	**ORGANISING** • Scheduling • Delegating • Budgeting **CONTROLLING** • Forecasting • Risk Management • Feedback	**PERFORMING** • Clarifying • Accountability • Consistency **ADAPTING** • Focusing • Mastering • Persistence	

CHAPTER 22

Learn to learn faster

"It is not the strongest of the species that survive, nor the most intelligent, but the one most responsive to change."
Charles Darwin

Solving problems forces us to learn and develop new skills. No two challenging problems are the same. They may have similarities, but will always have nuances to discover. This means we need to continually learn to develop our problem-solving expertise. The more we learn, the more problems we can solve, the more valuable we become.

We all have the capability to learn, it's just that some of us have learned how to learn faster than others. And with a little effort and focus, you can too.

Learning faster improves your intelligence. Intelligence is the ability to solve challenging problems by acquiring and applying new knowledge and skills. If you improve your rate of learning and your rate of retention, you will acquire knowledge and skills faster. Apply your new knowledge and skills to more challenging problems and your intelligence will improve. Problems make you smarter.

> **Learning rate x Retention rate = Intelligence**

When you learn something new, you effectively rewire your brain. The brain reacts to learning as a muscle reacts to exercise. They both transform when put under strain to allow growth to become stronger (and wiser in the case of the brain).[46]

The more consistently you learn, the more adept your brain becomes at learning faster. Like going to the gym, you don't get fast results by exercising your brain once a month. Consistently learning something new every day, even if it's small, keeps your brain in the mode of purposeful learning, which means you'll be able to learn faster when you need to.

Strategies to increase your rate of learning

Don't be so quick to claim expertise

Some of us are naturally confident in our capacity to learn and apply new skills, while others are the opposite and doubt our abilities, even when we're actually very good at something. Seeing and correcting your blind spots to learning will help you learn faster.

Cornell University psychologists David Dunning and Justin Kruger's research found that when we learn something new, our experience of learning goes through waves of confidence and competence. The rate at which we progress our competence is greatly helped by being objectively self-aware of our progress and persisting through the challenging phases of early success through to genuine mastery. The Dunning–Kruger effect, the name given to their findings, occurs when a person's lack of knowledge and skill in a certain area causes them to overestimate their own competence. It's a cognitive bias that's an ironic Catch-22. Dunning and Kruger discovered that people with limited knowledge in a subject often lack the awareness to recognise their own mistakes or gaps in understanding. They can't spot where they're going wrong and, as a result, they assume they're doing just fine. People with this cognitive bias don't yet have the ability to see errors they make as quickly and clearly as those with more competence can, slowing down their rate of development.

Here's an example to illustrate how the Dunning–Kruger effect works.

Imagine you and your colleague both decide to learn a new skill: facilitating business meetings. Within a few weeks, you're able to lead a meeting, outline key objectives, manage group discussions and dynamics, and find consensus among competing views. You're a bit disappointed, feeling you should have mastered more advanced techniques by now. Facilitating seems to come naturally to you, and because you grasp it so well, you assume it must be straightforward for everyone else too.

Your colleague, on the other hand, has just learned how to set a workshop agenda, invite and lead discussions. His sessions run a long way over time and allow dominant people speak for too long, making others feel intimidated to speak up. He's thrilled with his progress and believes he is now well on the path to mastering this new skill. However, he doesn't yet have the experience to recognise that he's missing critical elements, like managing time effectively and guiding discussions to include the views of all participants.

Despite having learned less than you have, his limited understanding prevents him from recognising these gaps. Without comparing his skills to others (like you), he overestimates his abilities and believes he's performing better than he actually is.

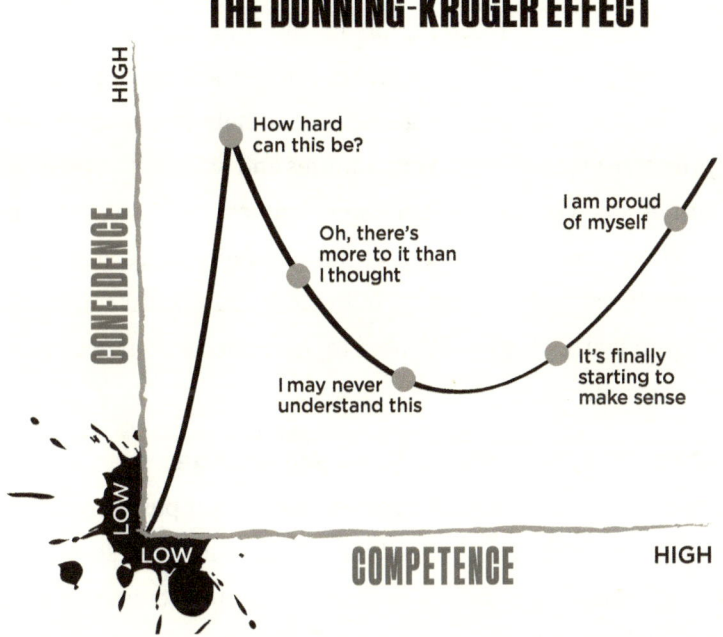

The Dunning-Kruger effect occurs because acquiring a small amount of knowledge in a previously unfamiliar area can give people a false sense of expertise. It's only as we delve deeper into the subject that we come to appreciate its complexity and how much we still have to master. Where people believe their competence is greater than their ability, this can act as a deterrent to seek out and learn more. If we fall into this trap, it can be tough to step back and realise we may be overestimating our abilities. Often, this means we're relying too much on our personal knowledge without seeking outside, credible information.

In many cases, the main barrier to learning is your ego. Nobody likes feeling incompetent, but trying something new means stepping out from your comfort zone and embracing the struggle of being a novice and adopting a beginner's mindset again. You'll need to ask questions that expose your lack of knowledge or attempt actions that might make you feel awkward. Learning requires being open to temporary discomfort. You have to trust that looking inexperienced for a short time won't damage your reputation in the long run. The truth is, learning something new *always* benefits you in the long run.

Recognising the Dunning-Kruger effect can help you gauge when to rely on your own assessment of your abilities and when it's wiser to seek input from others who can offer guidance on how you can continue to develop. Where you believe you have nothing more to learn, your rate of learning will naturally plummet. But where you remain confident in your ability to learn, or are motivated to learn more, then your rate of learning will accelerate.

Use impostor syndrome to your advantage

Being blind to our unique strengths can also lead to impostor syndrome. Impostor syndrome is the belief that others will overestimate our competence. This belief can exist despite concrete evidence of our past achievements or abilities. It's a fear-based belief that we will be exposed for our perceived incompetence. Some studies suggest that 70% to 80% of the general population have experienced impostor syndrome at some point in their lives.[47] Even some of the most brilliant minds in history have occasionally felt like they were frauds. Shortly before his death, Albert Einstein told a friend that praise of his work made him feel like an involuntary swindler.

Impostor syndrome shows up with behaviours and beliefs that make it difficult to take credit for your own successes. You deny your own competence, striving towards unattainable perfectionism and holding a deep fear of failure or success. This combines to create a self-perception that others have a higher expectation of your abilities than you do yourself. If you feel a touch of impostor syndrome, use it to your advantage. People with a bias towards impostor syndrome ask more questions than people with much higher levels of confidence.[48] Impostor syndrome amplifies curiosity, which enables you to learn faster.

Practice humility

Have you ever had a conversation with someone about doing something differently to how they currently do it and they've responded defensively by saying, "There is no need to change, we have been doing things this way for years and it's never been a problem"? When we believe we don't need to learn anything new, we become defensive. The antidote to this thinking is practicing humility.

Consume feedback like a high-nutrition meal

There's a saying that 'feedback is the breakfast of champions'. Be open to constructive feedback and resist the impulse to become defensive. High-quality feedback is a superfood for the mind. Feedback often comes in the form of criticism—comments on what you lack. There are two types of criticism: criticism that is designed to help you improve and criticism that is designed to harm you for someone else's benefit.

Learn to distinguish which form of criticism you are receiving and consume the one that is designed to help you—the nutritious type. Hand back the other type, just as you would a poorly cooked meal at a restaurant, because it's not good for you to eat it. If you feel vulnerable to the opinions of other people, consider this advice from comedian Jerry Seinfeld: "All this hand wringing worry and concern over how people are viewing me, someone said something bad about me, and you get so upset about it, is wasted time and energy. Your only focus should be on getting better at what you're doing. Focus on what you are doing. Get better at what are you doing. Everything else is a waste of time."

Strategies to increase your learning retention rate

Adopt multi-mode learning strategies

We can learn in a wide range of ways. The more modes of learning you adopt, the more knowledge you'll retain over time. Aim to use a combination of learning modes that work best for you. I've found this adaptation of the learning pyramid developed by the US National Training Laboratory helpful to focus on what I learn and how to best retain it.

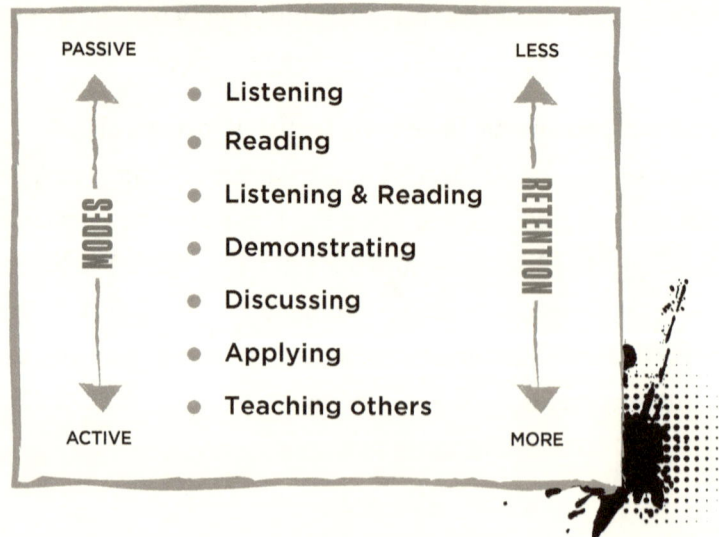

Where learning is mainly passive, we are more at risk of losing the new knowledge we gain the more time passes. Where learning is more active, in particular, sharing knowledge with others through helping them learn what you have learned, retention improves. Research consistently supports the idea that teaching a skill to someone else will improve our retention of it. It's referred to as the protégé effect. It's based on the concept that when we teach or explain something to others, we are forced to engage more deeply with the subject, and this helps improve our own understanding.

I found this when studying maths at high school. I became a tutor to other students by accident when they asked for my help when they were struggling. I found by explaining what I had learned, I was revising it at the same time. And if I couldn't explain it to them in a way they understood, I quickly realised didn't know it well enough. It highlighted my own knowledge gaps. Where someone else is learning from you, they ask questions. If you can't answer their questions, you have a gap in your knowledge you need to fill. It's a fast and free way to strengthen your knowledge.

Learn it as if you were going to teach it

Even if you don't actually teach what you've learned to someone else, approaching it as if you were going to teach it will significantly improve your knowledge retention. A study from Washington University in St. Louis in 2014 showed that students who were told they would teach others learned the material they were studying more effectively than those who were told they would just be tested on it.[49]

Forcing yourself learn with the expectation you will teach others will increase your knowledge retention.

Use spaced repetition

Spaced repetition is an intentional technique where you revise or practice what you want to learn at specified time periods. It's highly effective because it deliberately hacks the way the brain works. It forces learning to be effortful which strengthens connections between nerve cells, helping with retention of new learning. If you need to remember something you've learned, try revising it on day one, two, 10, 30 and 60. Spacing out the intervals to revise creates stronger memories of what you need to learn and locks it into long term memory.

Follow your confusion

Don't be afraid of confusion. It's a biological reaction telling you to find out more. Go where you are most confused. It's a normal part of the learning cycle. The faster you address your confusion, the faster you learn and lock in your new knowledge and skills.

Create visual aids and mnemonics

Use diagrams, mind maps or mnemonic devices to create associations and make information easier to recall. Mnemonics involve creating acronyms, rhymes, or phrases that link new knowledge to something familiar or easier to recall. For example, I created the acronym 3R to help people remember the problem-solving strategy (reason, result and response). They work by transforming complex information into something more manageable and memorable.

Mix it up and make it fun

Mix up how you learn. If you prefer reading, try listening to a podcast. If you like to take notes on a computer, try using handwritten notes for a while. If you like to write out long sentences to help you remember things, try creating a model to help you understand the basic concepts. Mixing up learning keeps your mind active and engaged. Novel ways to learn make it fun too. We naturally want to keep doing what we find fun.

CHAPTER 22

Learn to learn faster

- Learning to learn faster enables you to develop your skills to solve challenging problems more effectively, making you more valuable.
- Learning faster means increasing your learning rate and retention rate of new knowledge and skills.
- To improve your learning rate, become aware of your cognitive biases and take action to offset them where they cause barriers to learning.
- To improve your retention rate, adopt multi-mode learning strategies. Include teaching others or learning with the intention to teach others as a key means of retaining new knowledge and skills.

CHAPTER 23

Multitasking isn't always smart

> *"When you're trying to focus on something difficult, your brain can only do one thing at a time. Multitasking just doesn't work."*
> Barbara Oakley

My friend Ulrich Nettesheim is an organisational psychologist based in San Francisco. He coaches CEOs on how to build high-performing executive teams. We met many years ago when we both worked at EY in Canada.

Before he became an organisational psychologist, Ulrich worked on an offshore oil rig in the Gulf of Mexico during his gap year between high school and university. He needed a way to score some quick cash to help pay for his college tuition fees. Working on oil rigs seemed like the perfect idea. So, for a year, Ulrich became what New Orleans locals lovingly referred to as 'oil trash' (an oil rig worker).

With few skills other than an able body and a can-do attitude, Ulrich started working on an oil rig with shifts of seven days on and seven days off. Each week he travelled 400 kilometres to the oil rig in the Gulf of Mexico by helicopter, or in bad weather, by supply boats. Oil rigs operate 24 hours a day.

Ulrich's first job on the oil rig was working as a roustabout. This consisted of largely manual tasks, such as endless scraping and repainting of metal surfaces, refuelling various diesel engines, monitoring mud tank levels and loading and unloading supply vessels that brought everything needed to keep a 60-person offshore oil rig operating around the clock.

It was intense, physically demanding and, as Ulrich was soon to discover, very dangerous. There were literally an unlimited number of ways to lose limbs or be killed by the heavy industrial equipment. There was also the risk of blow-outs, where an entire rig can explode and burn in minutes, just as the Deepwater Horizon oil rig did in 2010. As an energetic eighteen-year-old, Ulrich thought he could make himself more useful and earn the respect of his fellow crew members by looking for opportunities to multitask. Doing more than one job at the same time, in theory, would make him more productive and valuable.

One of Ulrich's responsibilities was keeping the diesel generator that powered all of the electrical and industrial equipment on the oil rig full of fuel. The generator was massive—the size of four sedans double-stacked and parked end-to-end. It sat in a tight-fitting enclosed metal room with just enough space to be able to walk around the engine. The floor of the engine room also served as the huge fuel tank for the generator. The fuel tank had to be filled twice every 12 hours. At the front of the generator was an enormous cooling fan with blades the size of propellers on a light aircraft. Imagine the type of industrial fan you might see in a James Bond movie that could literally suck you into it and turn you into a finely chopped cubed steak.

On a pitch black morning at two a.m., it was Ulrich's turn to refill the generator fuel tank. Refuelling was something he had done dozens of times before. All he needed to do was enter the engine room and insert the nozzle of the refuelling hose into the fuel port recessed into the metal flooring, turn on the hose and let the fuel flow for about an hour. Because there was no fuel gauge or flow regulator to stop the flow of fuel when the tank was full, the person refuelling the tank had to keep an eye on things. The tank was full when you saw diesel fuel start welling out of the refuelling port in the metal floor.

On this Friday morning, Ulrich had an idea. "I'll let the hose run as the tank is filling up, leave the engine room and get a couple of other tasks done at the same time. I'll just remember to come back in about 30 minutes and check on the refuelling status", he thought. "Yeah, that's super smart", he said to himself.

Ulrich left the fuel hose running in the generator room and set off to complete the other tasks he had been assigned for his shift. He felt good about himself for finding a strategy to be more productive. Two hours later, with a flash of panic, he remembered the fuel hose was still running. His other tasks weren't particularly challenging, but required his complete focus to be done well. He lost track of time as a result and forgot to check the status of the refuelling.

Sprinting to the engine room, he pulled open the door, stepped inside and found himself standing in a 15 centimetre deep pool of diesel fuel that had flooded the entire engine room floor. With a burst of adrenaline, he quickly turned off the fuel hose and slammed the door shut behind him. He had a serious problem to solve. To save his reputation, he decided he would move quickly and clean up the mess before someone else discovered it.

Ulrich found a mop and bucket close by. Dashing back to the flooded engine room, he started vigorously sloshing the mop around in the pool of diesel fuel, wringing it out in the bucket over and over as fast as he possibly could. "This is going to be okay. It's slow but I'm making progress. Keep up the pace", he said to himself. As he rounded the corner towards the front of the generator, completely focused on mopping as fast as he could, he unwittingly edged ever closer to the enormous cooling fan. Suddenly there was a loud crack, and Ulrich was flung aside like a rag doll and left holding what used to be the mop handle in his hands. Everything was suddenly eerily quiet and pitch dark. The deafening roar of the engine that was powering the entire oil rig fell completely silent. Total darkness blanketed the drilling platform as every light stopped working.

Had you been sitting in a fishing boat a short distance away, you would have seen a massive steel island completely lit up with industrial lighting like a Christmas tree suddenly vanish into the night. In less than a minute, Ulrich heard shouting outside. Flashlight beams started darting around outside as crew members came running to the generator room to see what the problem was. What they found when they arrived was not what they expected to see.

Mop shards were stuck to the ceiling and splattered across the walls. There was two-thirds of a broken broom handle sticking out from the bottom of the fan attached to the nub of what used to be a mop that appeared to have been inexplicably jammed into the grating of the giant cooling fan.

If both activities you are trying to complete require deep thinking and concentration, there is little chance you can do both well at the same time

Ulrich was standing silent, motionless, hunched over in his yellow slicker suit and rubber boots in 15 centimetres of diesel fuel, still holding the remaining third of the broom handle. His mouth was open and his eyes stared blankly into the multiple flashlight beams, like an animal frozen in the headlights of an oncoming car. For a moment the crew were utterly speechless, trying to absorb what they were seeing.

If there was ever a sackable offence for a roustabout in the history of offshore oil rigging, then completely shutting down a million-dollar-a-day oil rig operation at two a.m. due to mismanaged multitasking would surely qualify. After an hour of feverish work, the diesel engine had been primed and successfully restarted. Most of the mop shards were pried from the fan grating and peeled from the walls and ceiling, and the spilled diesel fuel had been mopped up.

The foreman of the drilling crew sat Ulrich down for 'a chat' shortly afterwards. Luckily there were no serious injuries other than Ulrich's bruised ego and crushed reputation with the drilling crew. Asked to explain what happened, Ulrich said he was simply trying to get more work done by multitasking, but forgot to go back and check the fuel tank before it overflowed.

Surprisingly, Ulrich kept his job, the foreman thought the experience could be a learning opportunity (and a timeless story) for the entire crew. The crew renamed the generator engine room Ulrich's Cabin, and prudently relieved him of any further refuelling duties. Ulrich learned the valuable lesson that multitasking as a productivity strategy isn't always smart, particularly when the consequences are high if you mess up on one of the tasks. He didn't have good enough safeguards to make sure his most important task was completed correctly while he was focused on the other tasks.

Problem-solving often involves deep thinking work that requires focused concentration. Deep thinking work is not suited to multitasking. Research has found the more demanding the task, the more we become single-minded and unable to multitask.[50] Ulrich didn't put foolproof safeguards in place to remind himself to check the fuel hose. He assumed he would remember to check back on the fuel hose within the 30 minutes he had set for himself and focused instead on completing the other tasks. His intentions were noble, but multitasking in this situation was an unconsciously high-risk strategy.

If you're contemplating using multitasking as a productivity strategy to help solve problems faster, you might want to pause and rethink. If both activities you are trying to complete require deep thinking and concentration, there is little chance you can do both well at the same time. Science shows we can't outsmart our biological wiring—so multitasking isn't always smart. If both activities don't require deep thinking, then multitasking is possible with the right safeguards - like setting an alarm.

CHAPTER 23

Multitasking isn't always smart

- Multitasking as a productivity strategy is a myth where you have more than one task that involves deep concentration to complete. Science shows it can't be done effectively.
- Multitasking is very risky when one or more tasks have significant negative consequences if not executed well.
- Multitasking is only possible for tasks that don't require deep focus or when the consequences of lost focus can be managed.

Conclusion

Problems are abundant and everywhere. They are what we make of them. We can choose to see them as painful thorns to avoid or as golden opportunities to grab with both hands.

One thing is clear: problems will not leave us alone. In fact, they aren't meant to. Their job is to provide us with opportunities to grow, develop and create—if we take them on.

When you start to see problems as allies, not enemies, the internal barriers and limiting beliefs that can instinctively hold you back from embracing them begin to dissolve, creating a pathway to unlock your potential. We are all born with problem-solving instincts and our brains are wired to seek out new problems to grow and develop.

However, our conditioning from school, workplaces and society often encourages us to stick to the comfort and safety of routines, avoiding the uncertainty and discomfort that comes with tackling difficult challenges with unclear solutions. But the value of this as a strategy is severely limiting. Jobs are just temporary solutions to an organisation's current problems. Neither are meant to be permanent. What endures are the skills you learn and the capabilities you develop and continue to use.

Problem-solving isn't just a one-off task; it's a way of thinking, a set of perspectives, mindset beliefs, and a skillset that applies across all work and will always be in demand and highly rewarded.

Choosing to actively seek out and tackle challenging problems will transform you into a Problem Hunter, the most valuable person in any organisation.

Acknowledgements

I have been incredibly fortunate to receive the support and guidance from many talented and wonderful people to help make this book become a reality. Now that it's finally finished, I want to properly thank those who have made a significant contribution to it.

To **Sienna** and **Jasper**: my two amazing children. You were the inspiration behind me writing this book. You've shown me that doing really hard things brings out the best in us. I am so grateful to have you both in my life. I love you very much.

To my Mum, **Marion**: thank you for always being at the end of the phone with words of love and support as I've stepped through the joys and heartbreaks of life. Thank you.

To my dad, **Terry** and my stepmum **Nerolie**: thank you for your unwavering support. You've helped me stay steady when it felt like the world was crumbling beneath me. I'm truly blessed to have two such wonderful souls in my life. Thank you both.

To **Rob Colwell**: a former colleague, now great mate and all-round outstanding bloke. You've helped dig me out of the great depths of life I've found myself in more than a few times and have been a rock of support as I've surfed through the waves of doubt and temporary insanity as I journeyed my way from start to finish writing this book. Thank you.

To **Ulrich Nettesheim**: we share a kindred spirit of adventure for snow-based escapades. But much more than that, you've shared stories of your journey through life and the problems and challenges you've faced along the way and allowed me to include one of them in this book. I feel incredibly blessed to count you as a great friend. Thank you.

To **Jason Smith**: you've been a lifelong friend who knows me better than I know myself. We've shared some pivotal life moments that have helped shape me into the person I am today. I'm deeply grateful for your patience and friendship over the past forty-plus years. Thank you.

To **Iain Morris**: you're a champion bloke who was always ready to pick up the phone, jump on a podcast, be crazy enough to buy one of my artworks and let me couch surf in your office while I was writing this book. Much appreciated Big Man!

To **Pete Seligman**: your generosity of spirit, time and energy helped me centre myself and borrow the confidence I needed to take the risk and go all in to do something that was important to me. You were an inspiration for me to just go for it. Thank you.

To **Jacqui Garbett**: a lifelong friend and supportive force in my life. Thank you for helping guide me through the mess of high school and university and connecting me with my first shared apartment. We all need a guide at times to make it through life and you've been one of my guardian angels for the majority of my time here on this space rock.

To **Jeanette Gevers** and **Jim O'Donovan**: my amazing personal trainers who kept my body moving and my mind alive as I toiled away at writing this book. More than anyone, you lived the weekly progress of writing, worrying and inching my way through this learning process. You are two of the most genuinely wonderful people I know. I am deeply grateful for your unwavering kindness and support. Thank you both.

To **Rosalie** and **Gareth Akerman**: I am deeply grateful to you both for sharing your story of tragedy, hope and redemption. Thank you.

To **Rachel Drew**: your warmth, openness and generosity of spirit helped me learn in a much deeper way how compassion and empathy are two of the most underrated leadership and problem-solving skills. Thank you for sharing the gift of your story and life lessons with me.

To **Jon Michail**: for sharing your story with me and being vulnerable and insightful about your life journey and the insights you've gained from working with your 7,500+ clients. Much appreciated!

To **Marc Gregory**: your boldness, self-confidence and amazing story of creating a unique business that fits your passion and skills was deeply inspiring. Thank you for sharing the authentic way you journeyed from a career crisis to a compelling life for you and your family.

To **Colin Grant**: for sharing your beer baron story with me and kindly letting me gift it to the wider world. I wish you well on your future travels in life. Thank you.

To **Simon Dobbin**: for regaling me with epic tales of adventure on the Hollywood film circuit. I have never laughed so hard at things that were actually true. Thank you.

To **Sam O'Connor**: a seasoned strategy professional and epically clear thinker. Thank you for being an early test subject for my ideas and gifting me the use of your time and supercomputer brain.

To **Jonathan Dockney**: you have the razor-sharp mind of a lawyer and the practical sensibility of an engineer. I really appreciated your insights and support in the early days of working out what the hell I was going to write about. Thank you.

To **Christian Frost**: a man of principle and genuine care for others. You trusted me with challenging projects, were an early test subject for my ideas and graciously gave your time and support when I needed it most. Thank you.

To **Andrew Henry**: for offering me access to your vast depth of commercial experience and razor-sharp insights. I appreciated our conversations and the candour of your advice. Thank you.

To **Jessica Mudditt**: my wonderful publisher. You've managed to do the impossible and turn a hardened PowerPoint junkie into an author of a book with over 70,000 words. That is no small miracle. I've learned a great deal from you and am so grateful you've bounded into my life to help me with this quest. Thank you.

To **Bettina Kaiser**: working with you on the cover and graphics for this book has been a dream collaboration of artistic styles. I can understand why you are an award-winning designer. Your approach, humility, adaptiveness and creativity are inspiring to experience. Thank you.

About the Author

Craig Calder is a former EY partner, author, artist and founder of ThinkClear Group, a consulting practice that supports leaders and teams develop expert problem-solving cultures and capabilities.

Craig grew up in Melbourne, Australia, holds a business degree from RMIT University and is a qualified Chartered Accountant. He works from his adopted hometown of Sydney after having spent many years living and working in both Toronto and London.

Craig's journey from junior accountant and management consultant to leadership adviser, artist and author has taught him that the most rewarding and valuable work comes when you find challenging problems and have the courage to stay with them until they are solved. To not just stare at a problem and tell others about it, to do the work to find solutions and create change that matters.

Craig lives in the beachside suburb of Bondi with his two teenage children and whenever possible, heads to mountains for 'therapeutic' ski trips with family and friends.

Endnotes

1. A Problem Hunter's Perspective

1 https://www.hollows.org

2 Dell (2023).

3 https://www.3m.co.uk/3M/en_GB/careers/culture/15-percent-culture/

4 https://www.elixirstrings.com/my-elixir-strings-story?v=Products

5 Kegan, Robert and Laskow Lahey, Lisa *An Everyone Culture: Becoming a Deliberately Developmental Organisation* (2016), p 19.

6 Kegan, Robert and Laskow Lahey, Lisa *An Everyone Culture: Becoming a Deliberately Developmental Organisation* (2016), p 2.

7 Sourced from a CNBC article referencing a research report from global employment agency Indeed.

8 World Economic Forum, *Future of Jobs Report*, (2023) pp 28-29. They forecast between 2023 and 2027, 83 million jobs would be lost and 69 million created. This means they are forecasting a structural labour-market shift of 152 million jobs, or 23% of the 673 million employee roles they studied.

9 https://www.invent.org/inductees/josephine-garis-cochran

10 https://www.statista.com/statistics/1117972/major-appliances-ownership-selected-countries/

11 Author and global marketing expert Seth Godin in his book *The Song of Significance* reveals the reasons why people love their jobs. He surveyed 10,000 people across 90 countries and asked them to describe the best jobs they ever had. He found the top three reasons people gave was where they: 1. Surprised themselves with what they accomplished. 2. Could work independently, 3. Built something important. He found that people are most satisfied with the work they do when they solve problems, they thought they couldn't and these problems led to doing something that mattered. Doing this created meaning and satisfaction for those involved.

12 Catmull, Ed and Wallace, Amy, *Creativity Inc. Overcoming the unseen forces that stand in the way of true inspiration*, (2014) p x.

13 Lamott, Ann, *Bird by Bird*, 1994 p 21.

14 Ray Dalio LinkedIn video post 10 April 2024.

15 https://m.youtube.com/watch?v=L0L5t_1A-4Y

16 https://www.accesscorp.com/press-coverage/study-40-percent-businesses-fail-reopen-disaster/

2. A Problem Hunter's Mindset

17 Edward de Bono was a pioneering psychologist and author known for developing the concept of lateral thinking and introducing innovative methods for creative problem solving.

18 President Obama was interviewed and asked his thoughts on the most valuable advice he could give young people. This video captures his raw thoughts and illustrates how valuable problem solving is to leaders. https://www.tiktok.com/@coffeewithsimon/video/7248679418456050950

19 Medina, John Brain Rules: 12 principles for surviving and thriving at home, work and school (2014).

20 Frankl, Victor (2008), Man's Search for Meaning, pp 113–114.

21 https://www.ncbi.nlm.nih.gov/pmc/articles/PMC3746011/

22 World Economic Forum Future of Jobs Report (2023), p 39.

23 https://www.nationalgeographic.com/animals/article/predators-captivity-habitat-animals

24 https://www.psychologytoday.com/au/basics/imposter-syndrome

25 https://www.psychologytoday.com/us/blog/sustainable-life-satisfaction/201906/the-relationship-yourself

26 https://www.youtube.com/watch?v=Tfn6vD4yyC4

27 Instagram post (2024) @strengthinbodymind

28 https://www.mckinsey.com/~/media/McKinsey/dotcom/client_service/BTO/PDF/MOBT_27_Delivering_large-scale_IT_projects_on_time_budget_and_value.ashx

29 https://hbr.org/2019/11/why-constraints-are-good-for-innovation

3. A Problem Hunter's Strategy

30 https://www.psychologytoday.com/au/blog/the-gen-y-guide/201703/were-wired-take-the-path-least-resistance

31 https://journals.plos.org/plosone/article?id=10.1371/journal.pone.0310216

32 https://www.mckinsey.com/capabilities/strategy-and-corporate-finance/our-insights/fear-factor-overcoming-human-barriers-to-innovation

33 Sullenberger, Chesley, *Highest Duty: My Search for What Really Matters* (2009)

34 Catmull, Ed and Wallace, Amy, *Creativity Inc. Overcoming the unseen forces that stand in the way of true inspiration* (2014), pp 86–98.

35 https://www.myartbroker.com/artist-andy-warhol/10-facts/10-facts-about-warhols-marilyn-monroe

36 https://www.independent.co.uk/arts-entertainment/music/news/taylor-swift-taylors-version-albums-timeline-b2528845.html#

37 https://www.britannica.com/biography/Ernest-Henry-Shackleton

38 Shackleton, Ernest, *The Heart of the Antarctic*, (1909).

4. A Problem Hunter's Capabilities

39 https://www.thetimes.com/life-style/celebrity/article/richard-branson-virgin-atlantic-flying-interview-lfl9dspwz

40 https://news.stanford.edu/stories/2014/04/walking-vs-sitting-042414

41 https://www.health.harvard.edu/blog/sleep-to-solve-a-problem-202105242463

42 Land, George and Jarman, Beth, *Breakpoint and Beyond: Mastering the Future Today*, (1998).

43 Jonah Lehrer is an American author and journalist known for his work on neuroscience, psychology and creativity. He wrote *Imagine: How Creativity Works* (2012) which focuses on the science of creativity, exploring how creative ideas are generated and how they can be fostered in individuals and organisations.

44 Brown, Brené, *Dare to Lead*, (2018) pp 19-21.

45 Robert C. Wilson, Amitai Shenhav, Mark Straccia & Jonathan D. Cohen, *The Eighty Five Percent Rule for optimal learning*, Nature Communications Journal (2019), https://www.nature.com/articles/s41467-019-12552-4

46 Medina, John, *Brain Rules: 12 Principles for Surviving and Thriving at Work, Home and School*, (2014) pp 86-89.

47 Based on research by psychologists Pauline Clance and Suzanne Imes, who first identified the phenomenon in their 1978 study, *The Impostor Phenomenon in High Achieving Women: Dynamics and Therapeutic Intervention*.

48 https://hbr.org/2022/05/impostor-syndrome-has-its-advantages

49 https://source.washu.edu/2014/07/expecting-to-teach-enhances-learning-recall/

50 Simon, Herbert, *Administrative Behaviour*, 4th ed (1997).